An insider's guide to
Alonnisos

by
Julia Browne

Published by Travelleur Publishing
Denby Dale

First published in 2010 by
Travelleur
96 Thorpes Avenue
Denby Dale
Huddersfield HD8 8TB
UK

© Julia Browne 2010

All rights reserved. No part of this book may be reproduced, stored or introduced into a retrieval system, or transmitted in any form or by any means (electronic, mechanical, photocopying, recording or otherwise) without the prior permission of Travelleur Publishing.

The rights of Julia Browne to be identified as the author of this work have been asserted by her in accordance with the Copyright, Designs and Patents Act 1988.

ISBN 978-0-9556288-3-2

Printed and bound in Greece by
Printing Company, Georgiadis S.A.

The author has carefully researched all the information for this guide, but no responsibility can be accepted for any unforeseen circumstances encountered whilst following it. However, should you have any problems or find material changes to the information contained in this guide the publisher would be grateful for this information.

Για όλα τα ζωά

My thanks are due to Chris, who has given me such encouragement with this project and who has done all the nasty technical bits for me: my good friend Pete Hillier who has elevated my junior school artwork into a form worthy of a Turner prize: to those marvellous Sunvil and GIC clients who have been so generous with their compliments about the contents of my villa book: and to the people of Alonnisos who have made us so welcome on their beautiful island.

Iantha,

thank you so much for all your hard work. I suppose we have to let you leave, but come back any time!

All the best

Julia & all at ASAP

juliagicalonnisos@yahoo.co.uk

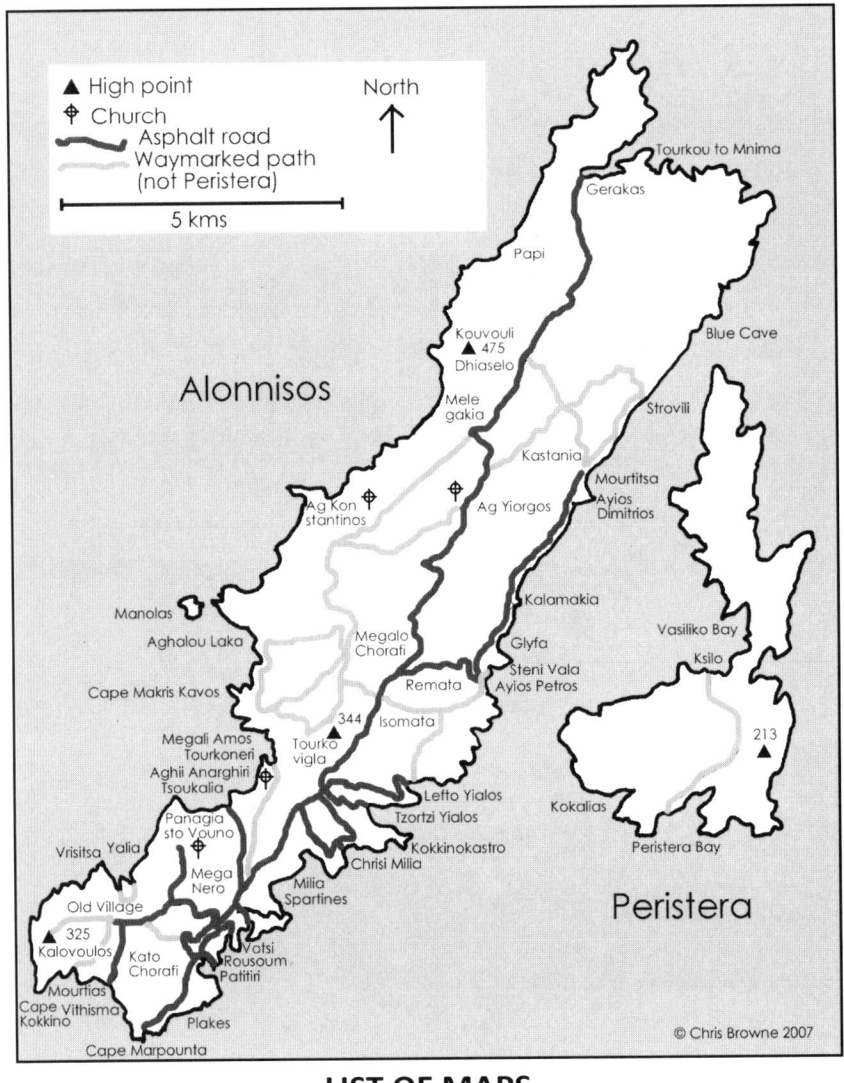

LIST OF MAPS

Map of Patitiri Town:	7	Map of Old Village	46
Map of walks	23	Map of beaches	48
Map of Patitiri: bars, cafes, etc.	28	Map of churches	72
Map of Patitiri: shops	40	Map of archaeological sites	74
Map of Patitiri, Rousoum, Votsi	44	Map of Marine Park	88

CONTENTS

Getting to Alonnisos	1
General information	5
Health services	9
Utilities	11
Fire	13
Safety	15
Transportation	19
Accommodation	25
Eating Out	30
Eating out: a glossary	34
Seafood	37
Retsina: an acquired taste	38
Shopping	41
Museums	45
Beaches	49
A brief history of Alonnisos	53
The Greek alphabet	62
Mind your language	63
Festivals and celebrations	64
Saints' days	69
Churches	71
Archaeological sites	75
Agriculture	77
Olive oil	81
MNMPANS: marine park	89
Alonnisis Society for Animal Protection	99
Useful contacts	100

The map of Alonnisos (facing page) is taken from Chris Browne's book "Alonnisos through the souls of your feet".

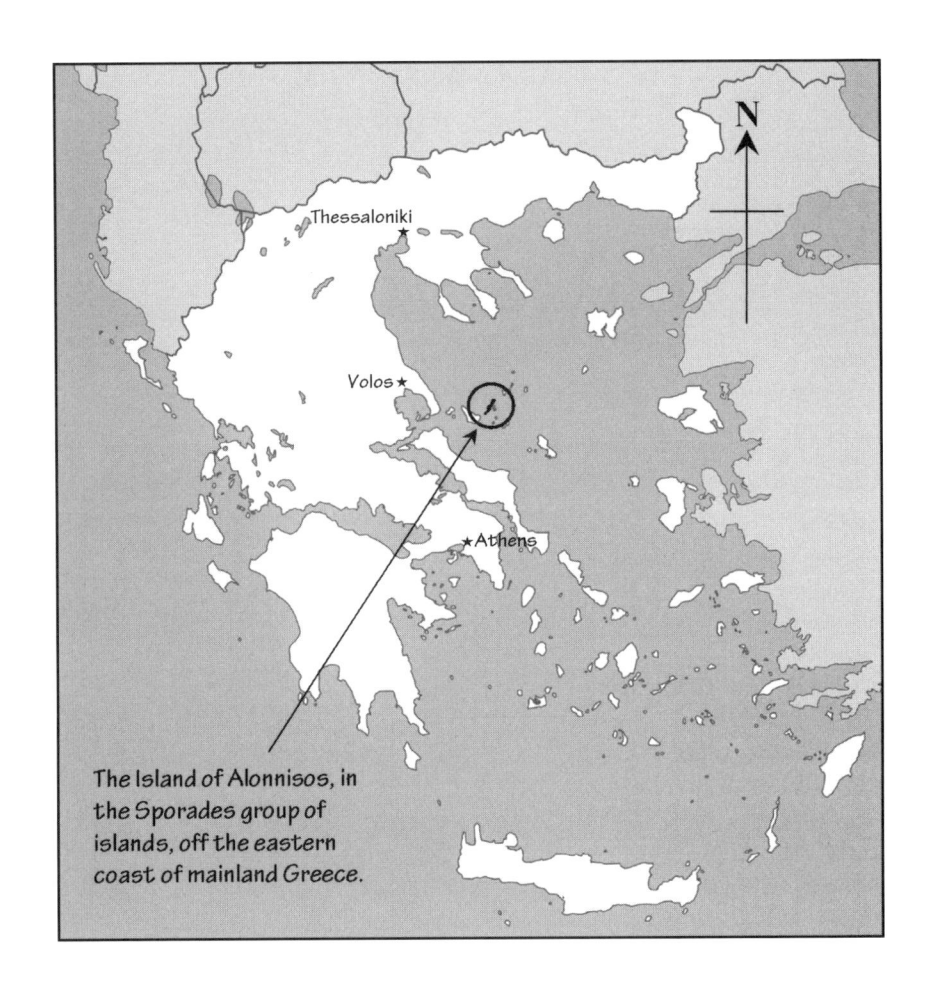

MAP OF GREECE SHOWING ALONNISOS

GETTING TO ALONNISOS

Alonnisos is a beautiful island! Spring is glorious and the island is carpeted with wild flowers. Easter is magical: the sense of community, the involvement of everyone in the religious ceremonies, irrespective of one being of the Orthodox faith, and the sense of a new beginning at the Resurrection is just wonderful. There is an air of expectancy as everyone starts painting with a vengeance to get ready for the new summer season. Shops and tavernas start opening and there is truly a spirit of camaraderie. However, if you are looking for warm waters, forget it! The sea is pretty chilly! May is lovely and June is generally pretty warm. July and August are very busy, with many visitors from Europe and mainland Greece. The Meltemi wind should kick in at about this time and this reduces the humidity but makes for a breezy time and fairly choppy seas. By September things are starting to quieten down and the start of the new school year means that many of the waiters in many of the tavernas have to resume their studies. However, the water has had all summer to warm up and the swimming is good.

So you decide – when do you want to come to Alonnisos? I will no longer give weather predictions! It seems to me that the summer has moved forward a month and the last few Septembers have been very wet, but I'm not an expert: just be prepared!

Getting to Alonnisos is not that easy: there is no airport, but that is probably a very good thing. However, it does mean that to get here you need to be prepared for a fairly long journey: it has been said that it is easier to get to Australia than it is to get to Alonnisos, but hopefully you won't be disappointed and will think that the journey has been worthwhile. Many people come back time and time again, so there must be something about the island!

From the beginning of May until the middle of October there are flights from UK airports into Skiathos. This obviously changes, but in 2009 there were flights from LGW, Manchester, East Midlands, Birmingham and Newcastle on Viking, Monarch, Thomas Cook and Thomson/First Choice. In 2010 Viking will operate a service from Bristol into Skiathos. From Skiathos there are ferry boats and flying cats or dolphins to Alonnisos (usually stopping at Skopelos Town and/or Glossa en route). These vessels are operated by Hellenic Seaways (www.hellenicseaways.gr). At the beginning of 2010 a new company, Poseidon, started an alternative flying dolphin service from Volos to Alonnisos. To get a comprehensive listing of boats, view the 'OpenSeas' website. It is absolutely impossible to give schedules as these will not be posted yet for the summer of 2010 and the schedules change several times during the season anyway. The only thing that I would say is that the earlier your flight leaves from the UK, the more chance you stand of getting a connection to Alonnisos the same day. And if you have to wait for a while on Skiathos before you get the boat, enjoy the experience! Have a drink or meal at one of the harbour-front tavernas and people-watch for a while until your boat is due to depart. You can book your dolphin/cat/ferry tickets on line and they will be waiting for you in the ticket office just outside the harbour gates at the port in Skiathos. However, if your flight is late and you miss the boat you have booked, the cost will not be refundable. The flying cats and ferry boats take a large number of people and you will probably get a ticket if you just show up at the ticket office. The flying dolphins have a capacity of only 120 seats and these may be fully booked by the time you arrive on Skiathos. When your flight lands on Skiathos allow for at least 30 minutes to pass through immigration and collect your luggage. The taxi journey to the port is only 5 minutes, but there may not be taxis waiting. Of course, if you book a package, all of these problems will be sorted out for you! In the summer months there is also a flight from LGW into Volos (Viking).

If you choose to come to Alonnisos out of season there are 2 options: flying into Athens or Thessaloniki. British Airways and Olympic Air (this is the new persona of the loss-making national carrier Olympic Airways) fly into Athens from LGW and LHR (BA from Manchester also). Easy Jet flies from London Luton and LGW, Aegean Airways fly from LHR only, but they are very good. It seems that airline schedules and destinations change frequently: please do no take what I say as 'gospel' but check for yourselves. There is a domestic flight from Athens to Skiathos operated by Athens Airways: during the winter of 2009/2010 this flew twice weekly, on Mondays and Fridays. However, the franchise for this route is up for tender at the end of March 2010, with Athens Airways, Olympic Air and Aegean Airways all bidding. If you should choose to take this option please check the boat schedules before booking, as flight timings might not mean that this is the quickest or easiest option.

From Eleftherios Venizelos airport there is an express bus (E95) which leaves from outside the terminal building and costs 3.50 euros. This will take you into Syntagma (Constitution) Square in central Athens. The metro costs a little more but also takes you to Syntagma Square, from where you can change lines if necessary. There are also plenty of taxis which line up outside the terminal: a taxi into central Athens will cost about 35 euros depending on the time of day (always more expensive at night) and the amount of luggage you have. Hotel airports are pretty pricey: there is a Sofotel opposite the arrivals terminal and a Holiday Inn about 2km from the airport. Obviously, there are many hotels in central Athens, ranging from about 50 euros per night (fine if you just want a bed for the night before an early start the following morning) to some rather grander establishments.

There is a connecting coach/boat to Alonnisos from Athens: every day in the summer but perhaps not during the winter. For tickets, contact Alkyon Travel at 97, Akamadias Street (www.alkyontravel.com). The office is adjacent to Plateia Kannigos, from where the coach leaves: on most days the coach leaves very early in the morning, about 6:30ish, so you might like to choose a hotel fairly close to the office. The coach will take you to Agios Konstantinos: the journey is extremely comfortable and incorporates a coffee-stop en route. It is important to book in advance. Of course, you could just take a taxi from the airport directly to Agios Konstantinos – about 150 euros – and stay there for the night if necessary and travel on to Alonnisos the following day. The coach service from Athens connects with the boat and you will be dropped off on the port, directly opposite the boat's departure point, about 30 minutes prior to departure. From Agios Konstantinos there is a 3 hour journey on the flying cat or flying dolphin or 5 hours on a ferry.

Another option would be to take the municipal bus from Athens to Volos (about 20 euros) but, again, you would need to take a taxi from your hotel or from the airport as the bus station is quite out of the way, on Liossion Avenue – you need to get it right, as there is another bus station serving the south of the country, and it is some way away! There is a comprehensive schedule and the journey takes about 5 hours. Tickets can be reserved in advance: if you do this by phone, you need to be at the bus station 30 minutes before departure time to collect and pay for your ticket. If you don't arrive at the bus station in time your seat will be released. A third option would be to go to Volos by train. However this is not direct – you would need to go to Larissa and then change for Volos. Volos is the nearest mainland city to Alonnisos: it is actually a very nice place to stay. Boat tickets may be purchased from the offices on the harbour front (Argonafton – the port from where Jason left on his quest for the golden fleece)) and there are more boats leaving to Alonnisos than from Agios Konstantinos.

If you choose to fly to Thessaloniki (BA, OA, Easy Jet), there is an excellent local bus service (78) which will take you from right outside the terminal building into the main inter-city bus station. This will cost the princely sum of 50 cents and takes about 50 minutes, passing through central Thessaloniki en route. The main bus station is the very last stop: the second to last stop is the train station and this is not the easiest option. Basically, don't get off the bus until everyone else does so! From the main bus station there are regular buses to Volos (again, about 20 euros). The same applies with reserving seats on the coach to Volos – you need to get there 30 minutes in advance if you reserve a seat by phone. The journey to Volos takes 2 hours thirty minutes and passes by Mount Olympus and through the Vale of Tembi. There are no stops, so you need to do the necessary before boarding. Only in late June, July and August is there a direct flying cat from Thessaloniki to Alonnisos – perhaps! Whichever route you choose, try not to see the journey as a chore, but an experience! At the time of writing (Jan 2010) there has been a major land slip on the way from Thessaloniki to Volos: this has resulted in a very long detour, so that instead of taking 2.5 hours the bus has to 'go round the houses' and takes about twice as long. Hopefully this problem will be resolved by the summer.

Spring flowers and Megali Ammos

GENERAL INFORMATION

BANK (tel: 24240 65777)
The main bank in Patitiri is the National Bank of Greece. Working hours are 08.00 to 14.30 Monday - Thursday and 08.00 to 14.00 Friday. There is a cash point, which accepts all the usual credit/cash cards. For exchange of traveller's cheques you will need to show your passport.

POLICE (tel: 24240 65205)
The police station is above the Taverna Leventis. I trust you will not need to visit this establishment: however, if you lose anything you will need a police report in order to make an insurance claim. Losses should be reported within 24 hours. Visit the station to give details of the lost item – they will then prepare a report and attach the appropriate revenue stamps (a charge is made for the face value of the stamps, usually less than 1 euro) and the completed form can be collected the following day.

PORT POLICE (tel: 24240 65595)
This is situated in the Kavos area of Patitiri, near the Paradise Hotel. If you incur the wrath of the port police by parking your car in a restricted area, such as the port, you will be issued with a parking ticket - this has to be paid at the port police station (the current cost is 80 euros).

In theory, you also need a permit from the Port Police if you wish to fish from a small boat (no permit is required for fishing from the shore).

The port police have absolute authority over what vessels can leave the main port of Patitiri: this includes pleasure craft as well as the commercial ferries, flying catamarans and hydrofoils. If the wind speed exceeds (or is predicted to exceed) force 5 on the Beaufort scale the hydrofoils will be cancelled and taxi/excursion boats will not be allowed to leave the port. A wind speed of force 8 will result in the cancellation of the ferries and flying cat also.

If a boat cancellation means that you will miss your flight, you can get an official paper from the port police office near the Paradise Hotel verifying the cancellation: this paper can then be handed into your insurance company and may allow reimbursement of additional costs incurred. Keep all receipts for extra accommodation, meals and transport.

PHARMACIES

There are 2 pharmacies on the island and these are situated along the main street in Patitiri. Opening hours are 09.00 - 14.00 and 17.00 - 20.00 daily. In May and September the pharmacies may be closed on Sundays.

POST OFFICE (tel: 24240 65560)

This is situated on the right hand side of the main street as you walk up from the port. Opening hours are 08.00 - 14.00 Monday to Friday. The price of a stamp for a letter or post card to anywhere in the world (outside Greece) is 70 cents. Post boxes are yellow.

FIRE (tel: 24240 65199)

The fire station is near the police station. The forestry fire department is in the same building. Forest fires on the island are a constant worry – if you should see any fires, please contact the fire service.

PETROL

There are 3 petrol stations on the island ('P' on the map), all in Patitiri : one on the left hand road leaving the port; one at the start of the road to the Old Village; and one on the main road to Votsi. Opening hours are from 7am until 10pm, although these times may vary slightly with the time of year. Please make sure you have enough petrol to get back to town if you travel any distance! All rental cars now take unleaded petrol, 'aymoleevee' or 'prassino' (green) in Greek. Currently, a litre of unleaded petrol costs just over 1.25 euros, although this seems to change almost daily (usually for the worse).

PARKING

This can get tricky in Patitiri at the height of the summer (June to mid-September). The safest place to leave your car is in the parking area near the 'pine tree in the road', at the top of the main street out of Patitiri, or on the access road to the ferry port. Parking in the main port area is not permitted, nor is parking on the quay in Steni Vala, from early June until mid-September. Between these dates there is no motorized traffic allowed in the

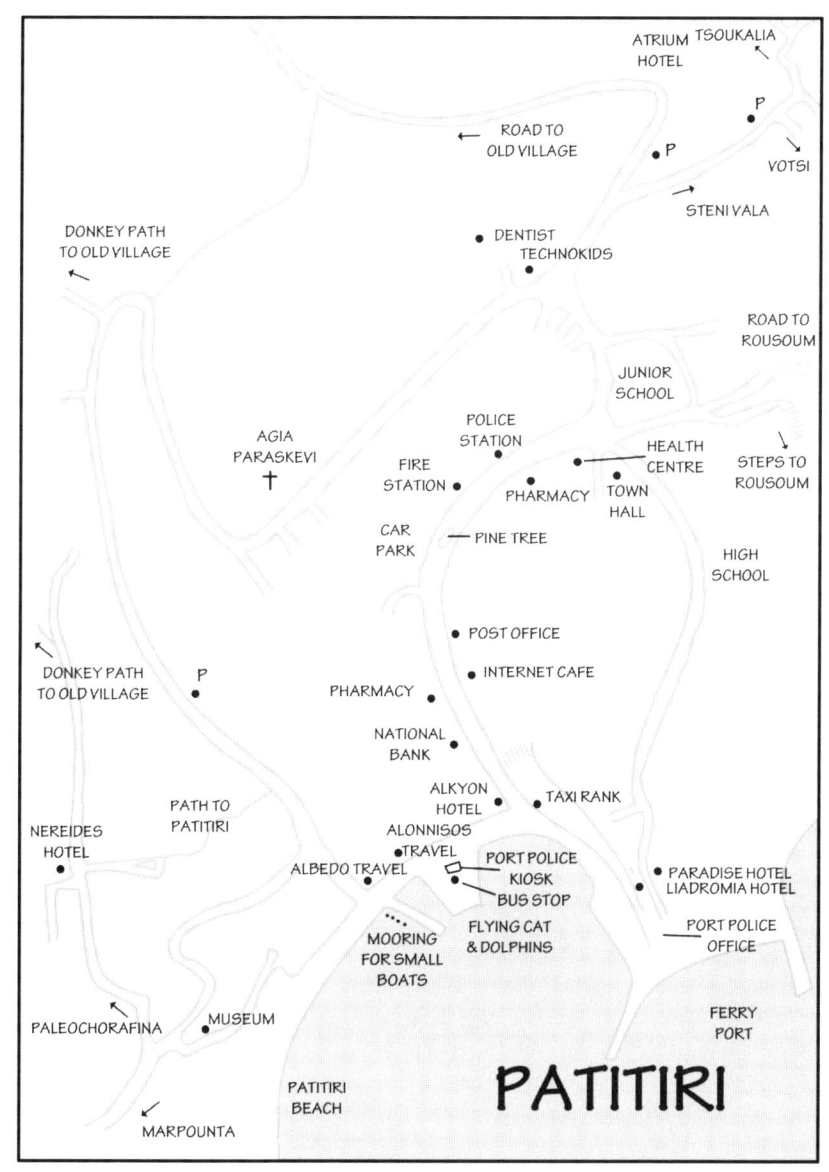

Old Village. In theory, there is also no parking along the main road out of the port – from the harbour front to the 'pine tree in the road'. This section of highway is the domain of the regular police: they are usually kind enough to give a whistle before issuing a ticket, but you have to move fairly swiftly!

TELEPHONES

Mobile reception can be poor outside Patitiri and especially on the coast. You may find that reception improves the higher above sea level you are. There are several mobile phone networks operating here: the best reception currently is that afforded by Cosmote. If you dial a local number from your mobile you will probably have to use the international code for Greece which is 0030.

There are now many public phones which take cards. If you wish to purchase phone cards (telecartes) for your personal use, they are available from the Post Office and from supermarkets at a cost of 4 euros.

Although the instructions for the telephones appear in Greek, by pressing the button marked (*i*) you can change the language to English. All local land line numbers now have to be prefixed by 24240, whether dialling from a card phone or from your mobile. The international code for the UK is 0044, and then the first 0 of the STD code is dropped. A phone card for 4 Euros will last for about 3 minutes when calling the UK - the cheap rate is from 10 o'clock at night until 8 o'clock in the morning. Alternatively you can buy pre-paid cards (Ya!) which give a much longer phone time.

EMAIL/FAX

There is Wi-Fi access and regular internet access at Technokids and the internet café on the main street in Patitiri. There is also Wi-Fi access along the harbour front in Patitiri and in the Old Village at the Panselinos restaurant near the bus stop. If you need to send a fax, the tourist agencies may be able to help you with this.

PASSPORTS

These should be kept in a safe place. If you should lose your passport please contact the relevant authorities immediately. For British nationals, the British Embassy in Athens is the issuing authority for replacement documents, tel 210 727 2600. As a precaution, make a note of your passport details (or better still, take a photocopy) and keep this separately. Some people email a copy of their passport and other important travel documents to themselves so they may be accessed wherever they are.

NEWSPAPERS

Foreign newspapers are available from 'Albatross', near the Marpounta road. The papers come to the island on the first hydrofoil leaving Volos in the morning, so are available at around midday (depending on the hydrofoil schedule). Please note that all papers are yesterday's, with the exception of a couple of tabloids which are printed in Greece.

EXCURSIONS

Different walking or boating excursions are offered to show our visitors the beauty of the island and the Marine Park. The best way to find information on boat excursions is simply to stroll along the harbour front and check out the boards of the boat captains/travel agencies.

HEALTH SERVICES

Emergency numbers are as follows:

Health Centre	(nosokomeeo/eeatreeo)	24240 65208
Dentist	(othontiatros)	24240 65616 /6937231812
Doctor on call	(eeatros)	6932489883

The Health Centre is sign-posted and is situated at the top of the hill on the right hand side of the road out of Patitiri, next to the Council offices and near the junior school. The clinic, which is open from 8am to 2pm and 6pm to 8pm (reduced hours on a Sunday), has neither a formal appointments system nor a reception desk (well, there is a desk but no-one uses it!). You need to make a mental note of who is in front of you and be prepared to be forceful in maintaining your rightful place in the queue. Don't be alarmed if you are in the middle of a consultation when several other people barge into the surgery: if your medical problem is of a sensitive nature, make sure you take your partner to run interference for you. Irrespective of how many people are waiting, emergency cases and young children are given priority. A doctor is on call 24 hours day for emergencies.

There is one dentist on the island. His surgery is situated on the right-hand road out of Patitiri, just before the turning to the Old Village, behind 'Technokids'. The dentist has an appointments system for routine treatment, but if you present yourself at the surgery as an emergency he will see you as soon as possible. The surgery is open from 9am to 1pm and again in the evening from 5 to 9.

For specialized medical treatment or orthodontics, the nearest facilities are in Volos which is 3 hours away on the hydrofoil. The Health Centre on Alonnisos rarely charges for treatment but, in case you do incur medical costs, be sure to keep any receipts for either consultations, treatment or medication to enable an insurance claim to be made. If you have an E111 form, stamped at a UK post office, this entitles you to free medical care in Greece. However, 'free' has certain qualifications, which I hope you will not encounter. Should the local doctor decide you need to go to the hospital in Volos, he will ensure that the hospital is notified of your arrival and that an ambulance meets you at the port in Volos if necessary. You will have to pay for transportation to Volos except in cases of extreme emergency. Should you need emergency treatment, contact your insurance company as soon as feasibly possible to find out what they will cover in terms of treatment and/or repatriation.

There are 2 pharmacies on Alonnisos and, if you suffer from minor problems such as topical infections, bites or allergies, or cuts and grazes, it is easier and quicker to go to one of these where the pharmacist will treat the wound (generally with a copious amount of hydrogen peroxide). He will also be able to advise you of the appropriate medication, often available without first getting a prescription. Homeopathic and herbal remedies are also widely available.

The pharmacy numbers are:

    Mahi Tsoukana: 24240 65540

    Kostas Klivas: 24240 66096   mob. 6944 580044

Both pharmacies are open each morning from about 09:00 - 14:00 and again in the evening from 18:00 - 21:00.

Alonnisos is also home to the Academy of Classical Homeopathy. This hosts a number of seminars throughout the year which attract homeopaths from all over the world.

UTILITIES

ELECTRICITY

Power supply on the island is 220v with 2-pin sockets. Please be tolerant of power cuts which, although not every-day events, are more frequent than in the UK. If the power should go off at about 8am (or earlier) it is a fair indication that scheduled work is being carried out by the state electricity company (DEH). If the power should go off at any other time, the first step is to locate the main fuse box in your accommodation: if the master switch has tripped out you can try to flip it back up again after first turning off all appliances. It is important that you turn off electrical appliances such as cookers and kettles as soon as the power goes off, to avoid the risk of fire should the supply resume while you are out of the building. The water supply in many properties is also dependent on electrical power to pump the water from an underground tank (cisterna): therefore please make sure that all taps are turned off. If the power comes back on while you are out and any taps are open, the water will start to flow and precious supplies will be lost. In addition, the water pump will run continuously, which they are not designed to do, and may overheat: this will damage the pump and increase the fire risk. It is always a good idea to arm yourself with a torch and/or candles and matches. If you stay in accommodation where the water is heated electrically, the immersion heaters do not need to be on for more that 30 minutes usually. It is advisable to switch off the immersion heater before showering as an added safety precaution.

PLUMBING

The plumbing on Alonnisos (and throughout Greece) remains a little unorthodox. As a general rule, please do not put paper or sanitary items into the toilet but use the bin provided. This is necessary for a couple of reasons. Firstly, builders here continue to use narrower drainage pipes than those used in Western Europe and there is the risk of a blockage. Secondly, there is no mains sewage network. All properties are built with a 'vothra', which is a natural septic tank. Basically this is a deep hole lined in a lattice pattern with limestone blocks. This allows a natural soak away and natural biodegradation of organic waste. If too much paper finds its way into the vothra then the pores will become clogged and the natural process will be impeded. As most vothras are cunningly disguised under terraces, the process of digging them out and doing something with the waste does not generally bear thinking about!

WATER
This is a precious commodity on Alonnisos. Your accommodation will have a large water tank somewhere, usually underground, and this is fed by piped water if within the village boundaries or solely by rain water collected over the winter months if you are staying in a more remote location. Although the water is fine to boil for hot drinks and cooking vegetables, bottled water is advisable for drinking. Another advantage of having bottled water to hand is that, in the event of a power cut, the water supply will also be cut off owing to the pump not being able to work. Few of us treat water as a something to be treasured nowadays, but here the consequences of running out of water are dire. As previously mentioned, only those properties within the village boundaries are lucky enough to have 'the Mayor's water': outside the village limits, people collect rainwater from roofs and terraces which then has to last until the next rainfall. If sternas should run dry, then water has to be purchased from privately-owned wells and delivered by lorry. As you can imagine, this process is very expensive (in 2009 $1m^3$ of water cost 25 euros) and is dependent on there being water available to purchase in the first place! If you could contribute to the island's water conservation by being careful with water then we would all appreciate this.

RECYCLING
Many people ask about recycling, but the simple answer is that nothing is recycled here (except beer bottles and the crown-corked retsina bottles, which should be taken back to the shops). We have one large landfill site where all rubbish is taken (I'll keep the location of this a secret, as it's not somewhere you would want to visit). There are rubbish bins dotted around the island and every type of rubbish goes into these. The over-riding reason for not recycling is the cost involved: all waste would have to be shipped to Thessaloniki and this would be prohibitively expensive. The vast amount of plastic waste is, of course, a huge problem and some hoteliers have tried to promote 'environmental tourism' by using fewer pre-packed jams, butter etc and fewer plastic bottles of water. So far this has been a drop in the ocean, but let's hope for better things in the future!

FIRE

The islands of the Sporades are densely wooded with forests of pine trees, acres of olive groves and dense vegetation. During the summer the ground dries, the pine trees lose their needles, and woody herbs such as wild thyme dry out: this makes for ideal kindling! The forestry fire departments are assiduous in their watch for wild fires and have installed large water tanks in woodland areas to be on hand at the first sign of a forest fire. But, once a forest fire has started, the speed at which it can spread is truly frightening. The natural oils in the olive leaves ensure that the trees burn ferociously. Similarly, the resin in the pine trees is hugely combustible and, once the pine cones are on fire they act like little bombs, shooting off the trees in all directions and starting new fires. Therefore we would ask visitors to the island to take care and observe the following:

- Please be careful where you discard cigarettes, especially if it's windy. Never throw lighted cigarettes from cars.

- Be careful when using BBQ's. Please do not light them in exposed locations or when the wind conditions make their use impractical.

- Lighting fires on beaches (or anywhere else for that matter!) is strictly prohibited.

Should there be a fire at your accommodation, the primary objectives are to remain calm, to ensure the safety of yourself and other members of your party and to alert the relevant authorities. The emergency numbers for the fire brigade and police are 100 and 199 respectively. If you are staying in an out-of-the-way location it might not be possible to alert the fire brigade immediately: in this case, your safety is of paramount importance.

- Make sure you and your family get out of the house as quickly as possible and keep some distance away to avoid being harmed by falling masonry or secondary fires.

- Tackle the fire yourself ONLY if you can do so without endangering yourself or others. Under EOT certification, fire extinguishers supplied are powder based, so are suitable for electrical fires.

- If you should become trapped in a burning building, shut any doors between you and the fire and put wet towels or blankets at the bottom of the door, if possible, to prevent smoke coming into the room.
- Never endanger lives by trying to rescue personal items. Stay away from the building until the fire services allow you to re-enter.

It isn't always sunny!

SAFETY

The following advice will hopefully enable you to avoid problems during your stay.

CREATURES

Leaving food out of the fridge is an invitation to **ants** and other insects: try to ensure that all food has been put away when you go out or you may have unwelcome visitors on your return.

Mosquitoes may be a problem in the evening or at night. There are a number of repellent creams and lotions available from the pharmacies which seem to be effective. Supermarkets stock plug-in electrical devices which vaporize an insecticide tablet, to enable you to get a bite-free night's sleep. They also sell coils and sprays to discourage mosquitoes.

There are **snakes** on the island but most of these are non-poisonous. The dark brown ones are grass snakes which are harmless and generally very keen on avoiding humans: probably your only contact with one will be when you hear it disappearing into the undergrowth in an attempt to get out of your way. There are also adders, which have the characteristic diamond pattern on their backs. These are also shy, but whereas the grass snakes will slither away when they sense something approaching, adders tend to freeze. The answer is to watch where you put your feet when walking through the undergrowth. An adder bite will not prove fatal, unless there is some underlying medical condition, but may cause some unpleasant side effects such as severe headache and muscle pains. If bitten, keep calm, avoid exertion and seek medical advice immediately.

Many reptiles can harbour Salmonella bacteria, so should be handled cautiously (preferably not at all!). This applies particularly to **tortoises.**

Rarely, **scorpions** may be seen. Avoid walking around in bare feet, and shake out clothes and shoes before putting them on. If you should be stung, seek medical attention immediately.

If you decide to sleep on or near a beach, it's sensible to use insect repellent to guard against being bitten by **sandflies**. These may spread a protozoal infection called leishmaniasis (Kala-azar), which is difficult to treat.

Urchins are to be found in rocky areas of the sea-shore: be careful where you put your hands and wear beach shoes when swimming. If you touch an urchin and the spines become embedded in your flesh, please resist the urge to prod, poke or pick at them to get them out. By doing this you risk infection: if you leave them, local inflammation will push the spines out naturally within a couple of days.

Periodically there are **jelly-fish** in the sea (fortunately no man-of-war species): most frequently these are the transparent blob kind (Moon jellyfish), which are harmless, but occasionally species of Cassiopeia may be seen. These look like fried eggs and do have stinging cells on their tentacles. They are very large, with a diameter of about 40cm, and are probably best avoided. If you should be stung by a jelly fish or a flying insect such as a **wasp** or **hornet**, application of a dilute acid such as vinegar or lemon juice will relieve the pain. Urine is also said to work, but I haven't tried this personally!

As far as I know, there have been no reports of injuries caused by **weever fish** on Alonnisos. These brutes bury themselves in sand with only their dorsal and gill spines protruding. Should you tread on one of these creatures

Pine Processionary caterpillar nest

the sudden pain is excruciating and permanent paralysis of the affected area may follow: it is important to immerse the affected part in water as hot as you can stand. This degrades the toxin, and relieves the swelling and pain: obviously, medical attention should be sought. Another good reason to wear beach shoes I think!

Stingrays and **skates** are a little more common. These frequent bays with sandy bottoms where they can bury themselves in the sand and then lie in wait for an eager paddler to tread on them. They are shy creatures but will lash out with their tails if trodden on: this can be very painful, so it is wise to make your presence known in advance by splashing around when entering the water.

Finally, in addition to being very destructive to pine trees, **the pine processionary caterpillar** has highly irritating hairs which, if touched (either directly or indirectly), will introduce a toxin causing skin welts and immense local irritation probably requiring antihistamine treatment. These little beasts are only in evidence early in the year.

And now a bit of good news - there is no **rabies** in Greece!

POLLEN

The Greek pollen season is at its height from April to June. The pollen from the pine trees is particularly allergenic and is responsible for a high incidence of respiratory problems. If you suffer from hay fever or asthma, please make sure you are armed with anti-allergic medications or the appropriate bronchodilators. If you have any questions or anxieties about the efficacy of medicines the Pharmacists would be happy to offer advice.

SUN

The sun is very intense and even when there is some cloud cover this affords very little UV filtration. At the start of your holiday please take extra care to avoid the hottest parts of the day, wear a hat, and use plenty of high-factor sunscreen on vulnerable parts such as the nose, neck and shoulders. When snorkelling or boating it is advisable to wear a T-shirt as the reflection of the sun's rays off the water intensifies burning potential. To avoid sun- or heat-stroke, drink plenty of bottled water and keep your body temperature down with frequent dips in the sea or swimming pool. Too many ice-cold drinks in the heat of the day may lead to stomach upsets. As you lose more salt from your body when it's hot, additional salt on food or the addition of rehydration salts to drinking water may help prevent cramps.

WALKING

When going walking remember to take plenty of water, sun-tan lotion, a hat and whatever food you may need. Take a mobile if you have one, although be prepared to have to move around to get decent reception. Torches are useful if you are walking at night.

SWIMMING

The seas around Alonnisos are very safe: the water is crystal clear and non-tidal, but currents may be quite strong in rough weather. Don't swim for a couple of hours after eating and, if you've been drinking alcohol, wait until the effects have worn off before entering the water.

Tortoise

TRANSPORTATION

There are reasonable tarmac roads which link the main port of Patitiri with the Old Village and Votsi. A surfaced road leads northwards and splits into two before reaching Steni Vala. One branch continues along the spine of the island, offering superb views to the islands of the Marine Park, and ends at Gerakas where the Biological Research Station is located. The other branch winds down to the coast and passes through Steni Vala, Kalamakia and Vamvakies before finishing at Agios Dimitrios. Place names are signposted in both Greek and English (sometimes!).

In addition, a series of graded roads and tracks lead down to beaches on both sides of the island: these are generally good, but care should be taken when driving. Insurance on hire cars does not include cover for shredded tyres or damage to the undercarriage.

CAR HIRE

To hire a car you will need to show your passport and a valid driving licence, which has been held for at least one year. To drive a hire car you must be over 23 years old. You will be given a rental contract, which you should keep in the car to show the police in the event you are stopped. Hire companies will not provide you with log books or separate insurance papers.

Greek law stipulates the use of seat belts and prohibits children under the age of 10 from sitting in the front seat of the car. Most car hire companies have child seats. It is also against the law to drink and drive. Surprisingly, it is against the law to use the horn except in an emergency or to avoid a collision. However, local exceptions to this law include expressions of joy at christenings, weddings, etc., trying to attract a shopkeeper's attention so he can bring you out an ice cream, or when Olympiakos score! If you wish to visit any of the other islands you will not be permitted to take your hired car with you.

If you should break down in your hired car, call the rental company straightaway and do not try to move the car: just wait with it until help arrives.

If you should have an accident it is important to keep calm. If there are injuries to yourself or your passengers, call the emergency doctor's number.

If possible, call the car hire company too. Passers-by can always be enlisted to help with telephone calls. If possible turn off the engine to avoid the risk of fire and move away from the car and out of danger from passing vehicles. If passengers are badly injured it is imperative that you do not try to move them. The car hire company will alert the police who are obliged to prepare a report of the incident: do not move the car as the police will sketch the position of the vehicle(s) involved in the accident. If they cannot do this because the cars have been moved, any insurance claims will be nullified and you might be asked to pay the full cost of repair or replacement.

SCOOTER HIRE

As an alternative to 4 wheels, several firms rent mopeds, fully-automatic scooters or low-cc motor bikes. The cost of hire includes third party insurance. It is actually law in Greece that a helmet should be supplied with rented motorbikes: it doesn't, however, say that this has to be worn. You may hire a 50cc scooter with a driving licence valid for cars, for anything more powerful you will need a motorcycle licence. There is a definite allure to riding around the island on two wheels. However, many of the graded roads are covered in loose sand or shale which makes it very easy for the rear wheel to take a different direction from the front. Also, after a shower of rain the road surface tends to become very greasy. If you are not used to driving a scooter, I would not recommend that you hire one here for the first time. If you do decide to hire a bike, wear the helmet provided. While no-one expects you to wear full leathers, dress sensibly. Do not follow the example of the island's young bloods and ride a bike with bare feet: shredded soles are not conducive to a good holiday!

MOUNTAIN BIKES

Unfortunately there were none for hire during the 2009 summer season, but there is every possibility that this will change in the future: if there are any mountain bikes available, they will be obtainable from those companies renting scooters. However, be warned - roads on Alonnisos seem to go up more often than they go down!

TAXIS

There are 4 taxis on the island and the taxi rank is on the harbour front in Patitiri, opposite the Alkyon Hotel. If you travel by taxi you can book your return trip with the driver: just tell him what time you wish to be collected and from where.

All four taxi drivers can be contacted on their mobile phones and their numbers can also be found posted in the telephone boxes. Taverna or shop owners will happily call a taxi for you if you need transport. All fares are fixed (not metered), for example 5 euros to the Old Village, 15 euros to Steni Vala. You should ask the fare to your chosen destination before you set off.

BUS

There is one municipal bus on the island, the purchase of which was funded by the Aga Khan's Bellerive Foundation. This leaves from the bus stop on the harbour front and goes to the Old Village, a journey time of 10 minutes. The timetable changes frequently, depending on the time of year, but a copy is always posted on the bus stop in Patitiri. The fare to the Old Village is just over 1 euro per person one way. At the beginning of the season the bus only goes in the morning: as the season progresses the timetable expands to include evening trips. From June to September the bus goes several times daily to Steni Vala. Tickets are purchased on the bus.

WATER TAXIS

From Patitiri, small caiques used to run a taxi service to the beaches along the south-east coast: unfortunately this didn't happen in 2009 as, I believe, there was a problem with licences. The boats started running at about 10:00 and the very reasonable fare included the return journey: the captain told you what time his boat would collect you from your particular beach. The boats left from the harbour front: the owners usually had a large map on a stand to show clients which beaches the boat would visit and it is at these points where bookings could be made. Hopefully 2010 will see the return of the taxi boats!

BOAT HIRE

Boat hire can be arranged if you would like to explore the small coves and beaches along the south-east coast which are inaccessible by road. The boats carry up to 5 people, are 4.35 metres in length and have 18 or 25 hp outboard engines. All boats are fully equipped with life jackets and flares.

They are supplied with 50 litres of fuel, and the amount of fuel found to have been used on the boat's return will be charged separately. Full instructions will be given prior to taking the boat out and you will be shown where it is permitted to take the boat. The boats are fully insured for damage and for third person injury. However, there is a 300 euro excess payable on insurance claims. Boats can be hired from Alonnisos Travel or Dimitris' boat and bike hire.

SHANKS' PONY

Finally, probably the best way to fully appreciate the immense beauty of the island - on foot! Alonnisos has a number of cleared and well-marked hiking paths. In addition, the island is criss-crossed by many goat paths and kalderimia (cobbled donkey tracks) which take the walker to those parts of Alonnisos normally hidden from view. Chris Browne's new book **"Alonnisos through the souls of your feet"** is an excellent companion, or you could join one of Chris' informative guided walks.

Gorge walkers

MAP OF WALKS

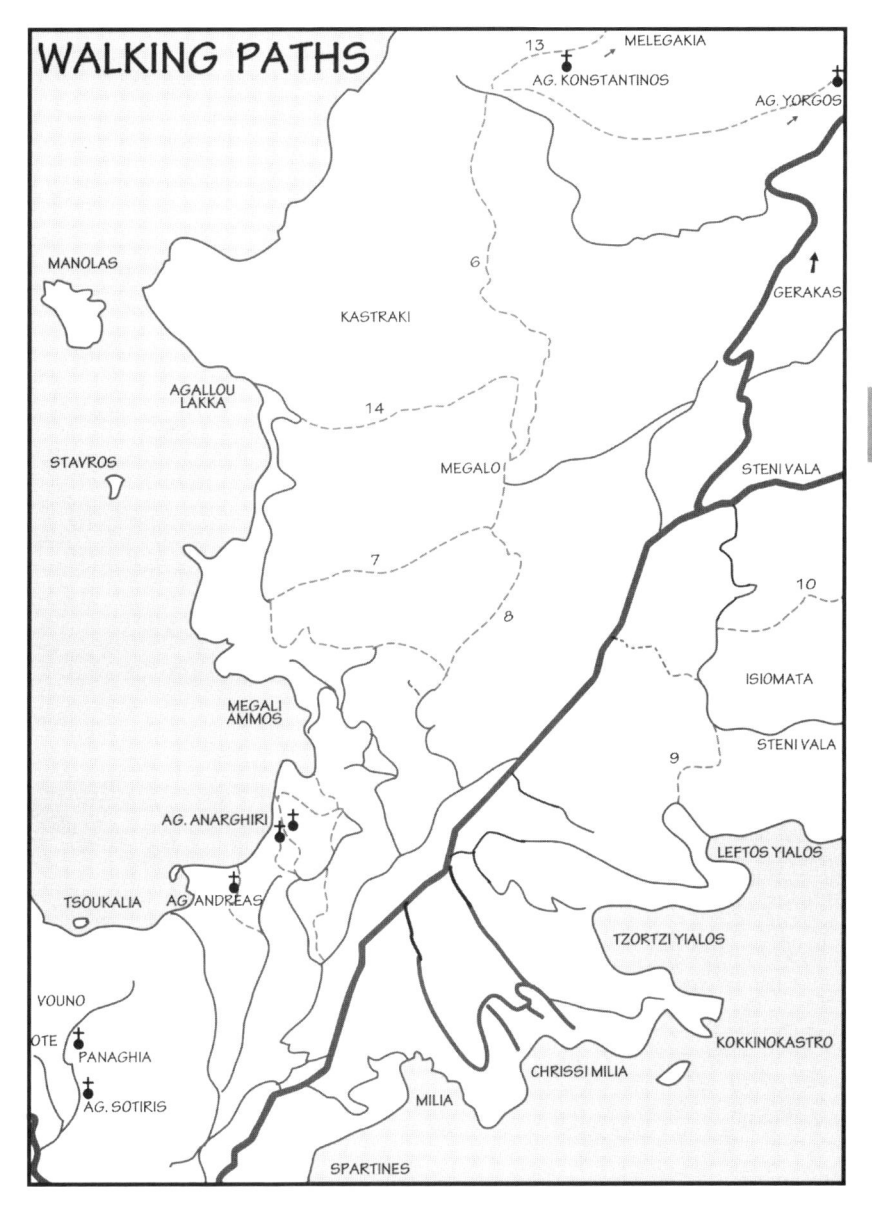

WAYMARKED HIKING PATHS

1. ALONNISOS OLD VILLAGE – MIKROS MOURTIAS (45′)
2. ALONNISOS OLD VILLAGE – KALOVOULOS (45′)
3. ALONNISOS OLD VILLAGE – VRISITSA (35′)
4. ALONNISOS OLD VILLAGE – PATITIRI (45′)
5. VOTSI – MEGA NERO – AGII ANARGIRI – TOUKONERI - RACHES – VOTSI (2HR 30′)
6. AGIOS KONSTANTINOS – KOKKINI AGORTZA – MEGALO CHORAFI – REMATA (2HR)
7. MEGALO CHORAFI – TOUFOTO POURNARI – MEGALI AMMOS (1HR 30′)
8. MEGALO CHORAFI – VATHI REMA - MEGALI AMMOS (1HR 15′)
9. REMATA – ISOMATA – LEFTOS YIALOS (45′)
10. STENI VALA – AGIOS PETROS – ISOMATA (1HR)
11. KASTANOREMA – AGIOS DIMITRIOS (50′)
12. AGIOS GEORGIOS – AGIOS KONSTANTINOS (1HR)
13. AGIOS KONSTANTINOS – XOURIA – MELEGAKIA (1HR 30′)
14. MEGALO CHORAFI – AGALLOU LAKA (45′)

ACCOMMODATION ON ALONNISOS

There are many rooms, studios, apartments, hotels and villas available on Alonnisos. Prices are lowest in May and at the end of September, with peak season being July/August. If you don't want to pre-book there are always local landladies who meet the boats coming in – they hold up boards showing the names of their studios and are ready to whisk you away if you want accommodation on arrival. There is also the rent rooms association of Alonnisos, which operates out of a kiosk on the main harbour front, opposite the port police office. The staff here will try to find you available accommodation to meet your budget. As an alternative to booking accommodation separately, various holiday companies (Sunvil Holidays, Greek Islands Club, Manos, Thalpos, Ionian Holidays, Aegean Holidays and Olympic Holidays) operate on Alonnisos and offer a complete package of flight, accommodation and transfers: you might like to check out their web sites which are listed in the 'useful contacts' chapter of this book.

Personally, I would not risk trying to find accommodation on arrival during the busiest part of the summer. The hotels and pensions mentioned here by no means represent all the accommodation available on Alonnisos – that would constitute a book in itself! Please check the official Alonnisos web site (www.alonissos.gr) and the 'useful contacts' for further information.

There are also 2 official camp sites on the island. Camping Rocks is on the Marpounta road out of Patitiri and there is also the Ikarus site at Steni Vala. It is not permissible to camp elsewhere, primarily because of the fire risks: please observe the regulations concerning beach fires, as the consequences of these getting out of hand are extreme in such a densely wooded environment. Typical camp charges are 5 euros per person per night, and 5 euros per tent (not supplied).

Out of season (mid-October to the end of April) there is limited hotel accommodation available and the majority of the studios are closed (they are not geared up for off-season occupation). The Alkyon Hotel on the harbour front is always open, as is the Liadromia Hotel in the Kavos area of Patitiri – but not much else. You may be able to find winter accommodation if you look at www.ownersdirect.com

A new concept for the summer of 2010 is the Alonnisos boot camp (www.abcrox.co.uk): you can book an all-inclusive week of accommodation, healthy eating, relaxation and an exercise programme including guided walks, yoga and aqua-aerobics

PATITIRI
Atrium Hotel	24240 65749/65750	www.atriumalonnissos.gr
Haravgi Hotel	24240 65090	
Liadromia	24240 65521	www.alonnisos.com
Paradise Hotel	24240 65213	www.paradise-hotel.gr
Alkyon Hotel	24240 65220/65366	www.alonissosmuses,gr
Nereides Hotel	24240 65643	www.nereides.gr
Pantheon Hotel	24240 65958	www.hotel-pantheon.gr
Ikion Hotel	24240 66360/65639	www.ikion.com
Villa Galini	24240 65573	
Pleiades	24240 65235	

VOTSI
Hotel Yialis	24240 66186	www.yialishotel.gr
Pension Dimitris	24240 65035	
Hippocampus	24240 65886	www.hyppokampys.com.ge

Votsi harbour

Vrithisma beach

KALAMAKIA
Hotel Agnanti   24240 66036   www.agnanti.gr
Margarita's   24240 65738

MILIA BAY
Milia Bay Hotel   24240 66036   www.milia-bay.gr

STENI VALA
Axilleiadromia   2424065158

OLD VILLAGE
Konstantina   24240 66165
Theodora   24240 65470
Eleni Tsoukana   24240 65135

MEGALOS MOURTIAS
Yiannis & Ria   24240 65737

ROUSOUM
Hotel Gorgona   24240 65317   www.gorgona.gr
Pension Oasis   24240 65098

MAP OF BARS, CAFES AND TAVERNAS IN PATITIRI

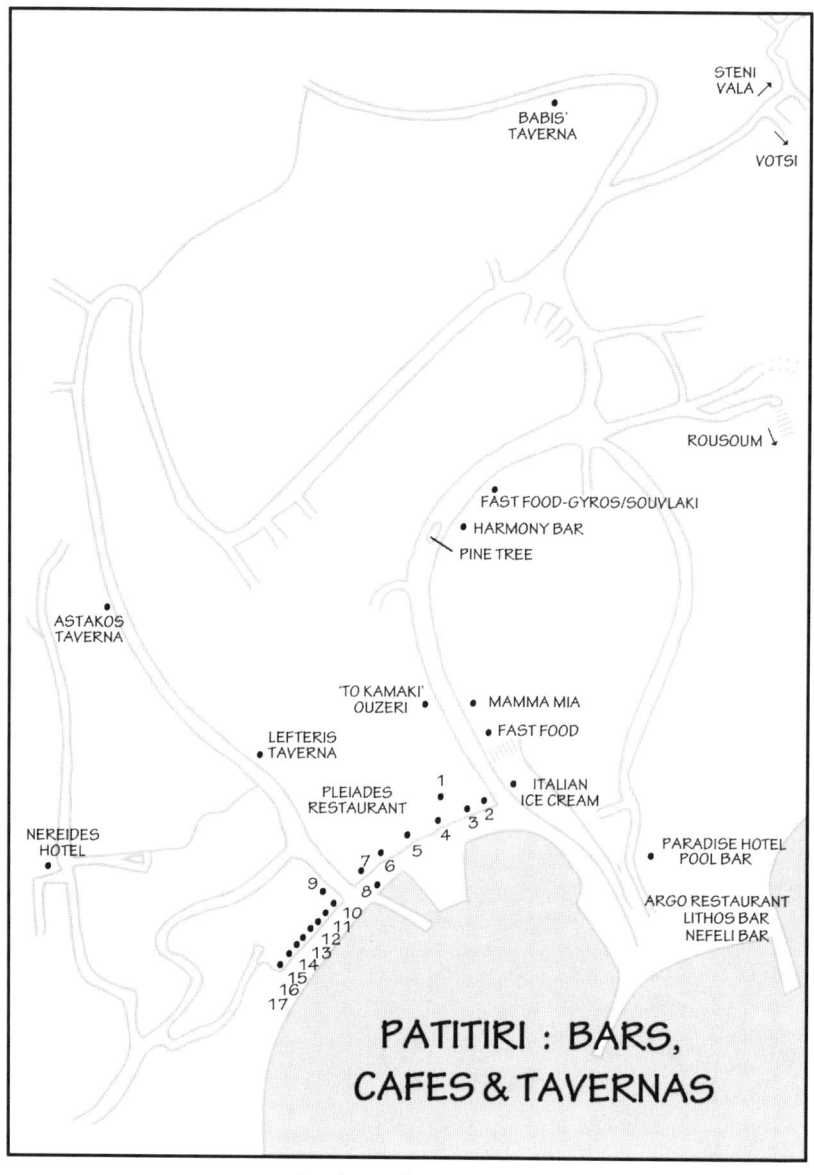

- STENI VALA ↗
- BABIS' TAVERNA
- VOTSI ↘
- ROUSOUM ↓
- FAST FOOD-GYROS/SOUVLAKI
- HARMONY BAR
- PINE TREE
- ASTAKOS TAVERNA
- 'TO KAMAKI' OUZERI
- MAMMA MIA
- FAST FOOD
- LEFTERIS TAVERNA
- PLEIADES RESTAURANT
- ITALIAN ICE CREAM
- NEREIDES HOTEL
- PARADISE HOTEL POOL BAR
- ARGO RESTAURANT
- LITHOS BAR
- NEFELI BAR

PATITIRI : BARS, CAFES & TAVERNAS

See legend: opposite.

PATITIRI: TAVERNAS, CAFES & BARS

1. RAHATI BAR
2. ALKYON CAFÉ/BAR AND GELATERIA
3. AVRA KAFENION
4. CAVE BAR
5. CORALI CAFÉ/BAR
6. ALONNISOS CAFÉ:
   DRINKS, PIZZA, PASTA AND ZACHAROPLASTEIO (CAKES ETC)
7. TSITSIFIA RESTAURANT
8. FLISVOS TAVERNA
9. 'TO STEKI' FAST FOOD (GYROS & SOUVLAKI)
10. ARCHIPELAGOS: RESTAURANT AND OUZERI
11. ANAIS RESTAURANT
12. MYTHODOS CAFÉ/BAR
13. PORTOLOCO CAFÉ/BAR
14. AKTI TAVERNA
15. AKROGIALI RESTAURANT
16. LA VIE PUB
17. EN PLO BAR

In addition to these eateries in Patitiri and those in the Old Village, try also the water-front tavernas at Rousoum, Votsi and Steni Vala. The tavernas in Kalamakia specialise in fresh fish. The restaurant at the Nereides hotel has excellent food and equally excellent home-made red wine. For a very pleasant lunch, visit the Sifanda bar at the Milia Bay Hotel. There are 3 very good tavernas on the beach at Megalos Mourtias: Meltemi, Taverna Megalos Mourtias and the Aegaio. There are 2 excellent restaurants on the beach at Leftos Yialos. The restaurants at Megalos Mourtias and Leftos Yialos are also open in the evenings and, for a good lunch, the taverna on the beach at Chrissi Milia is also highly recommended.

EATING OUT

The locals take their food seriously: the evening meal is a social event which tends to start late and last for quite a while. The art is to enjoy the surroundings and company as much as the food itself. Don't bother too much with the menu, this is usually a comprehensive list of dishes rather than an indication of what the taverna actually has on offer. It is customary to go into the kitchen to see what is available. The 'oven' dishes are prepared in the morning, so are probably best eaten at lunchtime.

Why not try the traditional meze at 'ouzeria' or 'tsipouradika'? For every small bottle of ouzo or tsipouro (this is a local form of ouzo, slightly less sweet but with the same distinctive aniseed flavour) you will be served with a small plate of food. This is a wonderful way of eating and the more of you there are, the greater the variety of dishes. Of course, if you are absolutely starving you may find yourselves having to consume vast quantities of alcohol before you've had enough to eat!

A word of caution about seafood: this can be quite expensive and is priced in restaurants by the kilo (the exceptions to this are gavros and gopes which are priced by the plate). Go into the kitchen or check out the display cabinet to see the day's catch. Select your specimen and ask for it to be weighed, then you will know how much it costs: this is preferable to being presented with a shockingly large bill at the end of the meal. All other dishes are very reasonably priced.

Before ordering food, decide how you want it served! If you order everything at the same time, it will come as and when it's ready rather than in the particular sequence you would wish. Oven dishes are usually served straightaway as they are pre-cooked and only require nuking in the microwave (or sometimes not even that). Freshly cooked souvlakia, meats or fish take quite a while. If you want appetizers before a main course, it is recommended that you order only these to begin with, unless you know that the entrees for your whole group will take some time to prepare. Please note, the Greeks consider it bad for you to eat really hot food, so be prepared for some dishes to be served a bit on the tepid side.

Desserts are not usually served at tavernas, although many restaurants will present you with a freebie at the end of the meal: either a shot of metaxa or a small cake. If you want a sweet something to go with your coffee or liqueur, move from the taverna to a café - you will also find that these establishments tend to have more comfortable chairs, which will probably be welcome after several hours spent on a hard, wooden taverna chair.

While you are here, why not try some of the local dishes? Here are a few suggestions. Kali orexi! (κάλη όρεξη)

SALADS

Marouli (μαρούλι): shredded lettuce, spring onions and dill, served with either a lemon/oil dressing or vinaigrette.

Horiatiki (χωριάτικι): traditional Greek salad of tomatoes, peppers, olives, cucumber and onion, topped off with a slice of feta and sprinkled with oregano. This will then have been doused in olive oil - if you don't want the oil, ask for the salad 'horis lathi'

Potato salad (πατάτα σαλάτα): usually served with a lemon and oil dressing.

Horta (χόρτα): wild greens, boiled and served with a lemon and oil dressing.

Kritama (κρίταμα): known in England as samphire, this is lightly blanched and served with a lemon and oil dressing.

Pantzaria (παντζάρια); a salad of beetroot with oil and lemon dressing. The beetroot tops are also included and these are delicious.

APPETIZERS AND MEZEDES

Feta (φέτα): this cheese is usually made from ewe's milk. It is quite salty as it is preserved in brine. If you order feta, that is exactly what you will get: a slice of cheese and nothing else.

Saganaki (σαγανάκι): this is a slice of hard cheese like graviera or kefalotiri, dipped in seasoned flour and fried. It is often inexplicably served with fried bread, which makes it a pretty heavy starter!

Taramasalata (ταραμασαλάτα): a mixture of cod roe, breadcrumbs or potato, lemon juice, onion and olive oil. This produces a paste and it is eaten as a dip with bread.

Tzatziki (τζατζίκι): yogurt, grated cucumber, garlic and dill.

Skordalia (σκορδαλιά): bread or potato, oil, garlic and more garlic. As well as being a tasty (if you like garlic) starter in its own right, this is a traditional accompaniment to cod and to kolokithakia.

Kolokithakia (κολοκυθάκια): slices of courgette, dipped in seasoned flour or batter, and fried. When freshly made, these are delicious with skordalia. Other vegetables, like aubergines (melitzanes), are also treated in this way.

Kolokithokeftedes (κολκυθοκεφτέδες): a mixture of grated courgettes, feta and breadcrumbs which is then shaped into a small patty and fried.

Melitzanasalata (μελιτζάνασαλατα): baked aubergines, peeled and mashed with lemon juice and oil.

Tirosalata (τυροσαλάτα): a creamy cheese dip. An alternative is tirokafteri (τυροκαφτερί) which is the same but spicier thanks to the addition of hot peppers (kafteri).

Gigantes (γίγαντες): butterbeans, baked in the oven with tomatoes, onion, garlic and herbs.

Fasolakia (φασολάκια): green beans cooked with tomatoes and onions.

Kakavia (κακαβιά): fish soup. This is quite a speciality of the island but it takes some time to prepare, so you usually have to arrange this in advance with your favourite taverna.

Dolmades (δολμάδες): vine leaves stuffed with seasoned rice and covered with an egg and lemon sauce (avgolemono). Sometimes these are made with a meat stuffing. Dolmadakia (δολμαδάκια) are smaller versions.

MAIN MEALS

Moussaka (μουσακά): layers of minced beef or lamb, aubergines and potatoes, topped with bechamel sauce. This is best eaten while it's quite fresh as it tends to become a little solid with age!

Souvlaki (σουβλάκι): kebabs of pork, chicken or fish.

Stifado (στιφάδο): a rich stew of wine and onions with either beef or octopus.

Pastitsio (παστίτσιο): macaroni baked with layers of minced meat and cheese.

Yemistes (γέμιστες): this means stuffed or filled. If you order this dish you will get tomatoes and/or peppers stuffed with rice (sometimes meat).

Keftedes (κεφτέδες): meat balls.

Soutsoukakia (σουτσουκάκια): meat balls but served in a tomato sauce

Bifteki (μπιφτέκι): home-made hamburgers.

Gouvetsi (γουβέτσι): lamb and manestra (rice-like pasta) cooked in an earthenware baking dish (gouvetsi).

Spetsofai (σπέτσοφαι): this is a speciality of the Pelion - country sausage cooked with green peppers, tomatoes and onion.

Prawn or mussel saganaki (γαρίδες/μυδιά σαγανάκι): seafood baked in a tomato and herb sauce with melted feta on the top. Beware – occasionally the prawns come complete with shells, which makes for a bit of a messy meal, but absolutely delicious.

Astakomakaronada (αστακομακαρονάδα): lobster and spaghetti in a red sauce.

CAKES AND PASTRIES
Baklava (μπακλαβάς): filo pastry, honey and almonds

Kataifi (καταίφι): nuts and honey in shredded pastry

Galactopita (γαλακτόπιτα): baked milk pudding in filo pastry, sprinkled with cinnamon

Karidopita (καρυδόπιτα): walnut cake drenched in honey

And finally, mention must be made of the island's speciality: Alonnisos cheese pie, tiropita (τυρόπιτα). This is filo pastry with crumbled feta (and sometimes horta or spinach, in which case it's called spanakopita - σπανακόπιτα). The pastry is rolled, twisted into a spiral and fried. These are absolutely delicious but huge - each tiropita should really be shared! It is well worth watching the local ladies making these. They start off with a tiny ball of pastry dough, which is then rolled out over a round board with a rolling pin like a broomstick. The pastry has to be stretched until it is the same size as the board: quite an achievement and a procedure requiring the utmost skill and patience. As they are always made freshly to order in tavernas, you may have to wait a while for the finished article - your patience will, however, be rewarded!

EATING OUT: A GLOSSARY

Eating out in Greece need not be a lottery: you might not know the right word to ask for what you want, but often things are on display so you have a pretty good idea of what you are getting! Here are just a few words and terms to, hopefully, ensure you don't starve while staying here. If you have any allergies or food intolerances I would recommend that you write down or learn to say what it is you can't eat (in Greek) so that you can check with the waiters before you order: say 'then bor**o** na fa**o**……' (I can't eat……).

If you should bother to look at a menu, restaurants are obliged to say whether the food is fresh or frozen. Unfortunately kalamari (squid) is now usually frozen owing to over-fishing locally and lamb will probably also be frozen. Most other meats and fish are fresh and, as such, are only available in season. Gavros, delicious small fish (anchovies) cooked like whitebait, are not available when there's a full moon: honestly – they swim deeper when there is so much light on the water and are less easily caught.

Cask wine is sold by weight rather than by volume, so you should ask for **e**na kil**o** (a litre) or mis**o** kil**o** (half a litre). In some places wine is also sold by the glass (**e**na potiri).

Achladi	αχλάδι	pear
Alevri	αλεύρι	flour
Amigthala	αμύγδαλα	almonds
Ag**ou**ri	αγγούρι	cucumber
Alati	αλάτι	salt
Anithos	άνηθοσ	dill
Arak**a**s	αρακάς	peas
Arn**i**	αρνί	lamb
Avg**a**	αυγά	eggs
Bougatsa	μπουγάτσα	cream-filled filo pastries
Eliolatho	ελαιόλαδο	olive oil
Eli**e**s	ελιές	olives
Exochik**o**	εξοχικό	marinated lamb or goat, baked in paper
Gala	γάλα	milk
Galop**ou**lo	γαλοπούλο	turkey
Yia**ou**rti	γιαούρτι	yogurt

Kalamb**o**ki	καλαμπόκι	sweet corn, also bread made from this
Kan**e**lla	κανέλλα	cinnamon
Karp**ou**zi	καρπούζι	water melon, huge and sold by the kg
Karvoun**a**	καρβουνά	anything cooked over charcoal
Kats**i**ki	κατσίκι	young goat, the elderly variety is Gida
Keem**a**	κιμά	mince, usually beef
Keem**o**s	χυμός	juice
Kirin**o**	χιρινό	pork
Kokkinist**o**	κοκκινιστό	beef or chicken cooked with tomato (hence the red colour)
Kokor**e**tsi	κοκορέτσι	lamb offal spiked with garlic and spit-roasted
Kolok**i**thia	κολοκύθια	courgettes
Kot**o**poulo	κοτόπουλο	chicken
Kounoup**i**thi	κουνουπίδι	cauliflower
Kras**i**	κρασί	wine: erythr**o**s/k**o**kkino-red, lefk**o**s/**a**spro - white
Krem**i**dia	κρεμμύδια	onions (spring onions are kremidakia)
L**a**thi	λάδι	oil
L**a**thera	λάδερα	oven dishes, cooked in oil
Loukoum**a**thes	λουκουμάδες	ball-shaped fried doughnuts, often served after a meal
Makar**o**nia	μακαρόνια	spaghetti
Manit**a**ria	μανιτάρια	mushrooms
M**e**li	μέλι	honey
Mil**o**	μυλό	apple
Mosk**a**ri	μοσχάρι	beef
Ner**a**ntzi	νεράτζι	bitter orange preserve, only found at the Ladies' co-op
Ner**o**	νερό	water
N**e**scafe (Nes)	νες	instant coffee
P**a**gos	πάγος	ice
Pagot**o**	παγωτό	ice cream
Paid**a**kia	παιδάκια	lamb chops, rubbed with salt and oregano and char-grilled
Pat**a**tes	πατάτας	potatoes
Pep**o**ni	πεπόνι	honeydew melon
Piperi**e**s	πιπεριές	green peppers (the red variety are florin**e**s)

Psit**o**	ψητός	roasted
Psom**i**	ψωμί	bread
Rigani	ρίγανι	oregano
Sk**a**ras	σκάρας	grilled
Skord**o**	σκορδό	garlic
S**ou**vla	σούβλα	meats roasted on a spit
Souvl**a**ki	σουβλάκι	pieces of meat on a skewer
Span**a**ki	σπανάκι	spinach
Spitik**o**	σπιτικό	food prepared at home, home cooking
Sto fourn**o**	στο φουρνό	dishes cooked in the oven
Tiganit**e**s	τιγανιτές	fried
Tost	τοστ	toasted sandwich, usually ham and cheese
Ty**ri**	τυρί	cheese
Tis **o**ras	τις ώρας	dishes cooked to order
V**o**tana	βότανα	wild herbs
V**ou**tiro	βούτυρο	butter (not usually provided with bread at a meal)
Vrast**o**	βραστό	boiled
Kseethee	ξύδι	vinegar
Zachari	ζάχαρι	sugar

SEAFOOD

Astakos	αστακός	lobster
Bakaliaros	μπακαλιάρος	cod, usually served with skordalia
Barbounia	μπαρμπούνι	red mullet
Fagri	φάγρι	sea bream
Galeos	γάλεος	shark or dog fish
Garides	γαρίδες	prawns or shrimp
Gavros	γαύρος	anchovy, either served cold in a vinegar dressing or fried like whitebait
Glossa	γλώσσα	sole
Gopes	γόπες	small sea bream, 2 or 3 per portion
Xtapodi	χταπόδι	octopus, either grilled or served as a stew (stifado) with whole, tiny onions
Kalamari	καλαμάρι	squid, either served in pieces and fried or whole, stuffed with feta and peppers
Karavida	καραβίδα	crayfish
Kolios	κολιός	chub mackerel
Lithrini	λιθρίνι	Pandora sea bream
Maritha	μαρίδα	whitebait
Melanouri	μελανούρι	black tail
Mithia	μύδια	mussels
Perka	πέρκα	perch
Pestrofa	πέστροφα	trout
Plaki	πλάκι	white fish, oven baked in a tomato sauce
Renga	ρέγγα	smoked herring in oil
Rofos	ρόφος	grouper, used primarily to make soup
Sartheles	σαρδέλες	sardines
Savrithi	σαυρίδι	mackerel
Solomos	σόλομος	salmon
Soupia	σούπια	cuttlefish, often cooked with spinach
Ksifias	ξιφίας	swordfish
Tonnos	τόννος	tuna, either grilled as a steak or served cold as an appetiser with chopped onions. Alonnisos bottled tuna, available from the ladies' co-op, is very famous.

RETSINA - AN ACQUIRED TASTE!

Greece has been exporting retsina for over 2000 years. According to Vassilis Kourtakis, managing director of the market leader in retsina sales, "the ancient Greeks knew that air was the main enemy of wine. They used pine resin to seal the tops of the amphorae in which wine was stored and shipped."

Retsina was the traditional wine of Athens: savatiano grapes thrive in the hot, arid climate of Attica and the abundant pine trees in the region provide endless resin. As Athens gained prominence within modern Greece, so the association of Greek wine with 'resination' also developed. Athens continued to grow virtually on top of the largest Greek vineyard and as most early 20 century visitors to Greece spent a significant amount of time in Athens, they were exposed to the locally produced wine.

By 1880, Athens boasted around 6,000 tavernas, all of which had wine casks stacked in full view of their patrons. However, because of the proximity of the vineyards to the city, it was the grape must that was supplied to the tavernas rather than the product of fermentation. As late as 1930 grape must was transported to the city by single and double horse-drawn carts. The size of the cask each cart could carry, and therefore the sizes found in tavernas, was determined by the animals' strength: 590 litres for a single horse and 1,190 litres for a two-horse cart. For many years after motorised transport was introduced the larger casks were still known as dikaro (two-cart).

Once a taverna cask was filled, the owner would add resin, wait for fermentation to finish and decide when to seal the cask, often by covering it with plaster. Wine drawn for the first time from a tap near the bottom of the full cask was called yematari (the full one). Wine drawn from a cask less than half full was known as sosma (the end).

Prior to each harvest, the empty casks were taken out into the street so that their 'faces', or side staves, could be removed, scrubbed, reassembled and disinfected with sulphur sticks (a combination of sulphur and paraffin). The sticks were lit and dropped into the casks before they were sealed: the sulphur vapours inside the cask would then kill any bacteria in the wood.

This on-site fermentation of grape must came to an end in the 1960's, as a large-scale migration of people from the provinces into Athens resulted in the demolition of the old style tavernas in favour of multi-storey apartment blocks. As tourism became Greece's largest source of income, bottled retsina replaced the old casks.

Bottled retsina also became available outside Athens for the first time in the 1960's. It was cheap and on remote, barren islands it was often the only wine available. Consumption climbed into millions of bottles, exports soared and Greek wine became synonymous with resinated wine around the world.

Attica's vineyard covered 120,000 stremata (12,000 hectares) in 1960. Today the area has been reduced by half and consumption of retsina is in free fall. The new Athens international airport at Spata has replaced a prime vineyard area and the commercial development that it is encouraging will further accelerate the decline of retsina.

Nowadays, the only tavernas which receive grape must in the traditional way are situated in the Plaka, beneath the acropolis. However, it seems that the primary value of retsina is now as part of folk-lore as non-Greeks drink it more than the locals!

Modern retsina is much less-heavily resinated that it used to be, but it still has its distinctive palate-cooling effect. In fact, no unresinated wine can match, much less complement, strongly-flavoured dishes such as gavros (anchovies) or bakaliaros skordalia (cod with garlic sauce).

Taverna retsina can be delicious, but inappropriate storage conditions during hot summer months can lead to container-drawn retsina being easily oxidised and ruined. However, cask retsina served by weight in aluminium jugs is evocative of balmy evenings, fresh food, amazing scenery and good company. If you prefer to play it a little safer, bottled retsina guarantees good quality and prices are reasonable. It is available as corked 750ml bottles or crown-corked 500ml bottles (this is perhaps a more local approach). Retsina is classified as a vin de table and designated an Appellation by Tradition.

MAP OF PATITIRI: SHOPPING

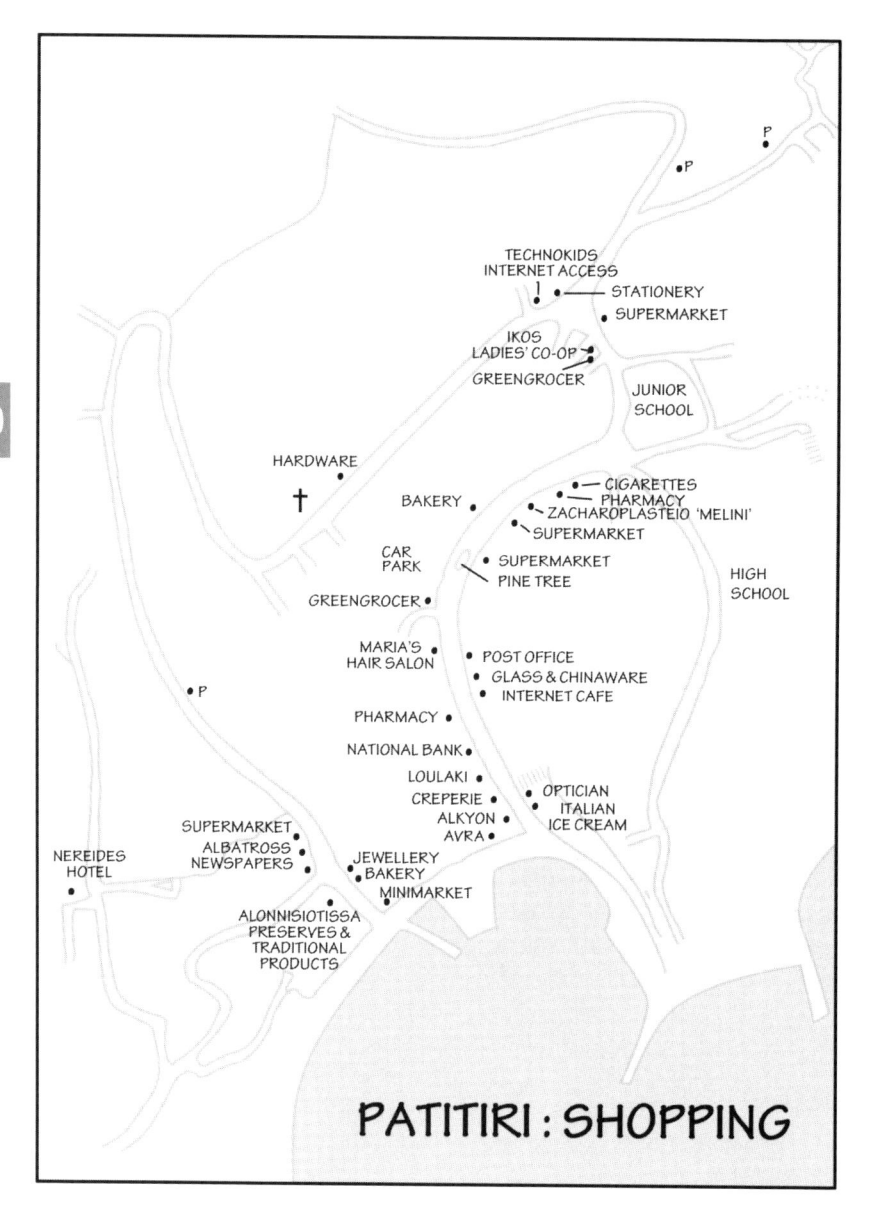

SHOPPING

There are shops in the main town of Patitiri and in Votsi, the Old Village (Chora) and Steni Vala. While Alonnisos is not over-endowed with shops, most of the basics are available. For more advanced retail-therapy you might like to consider a trip to Skopelos, Skiathos or perhaps Volos. This is the nearest mainland city to the islands of the Sporades and is situated at the top of the Pagassitic Gulf near Mount Pelion (a journey of 3 hours by flying dolphin or flying cat). In addition to a wide range of shops, Volos boasts a fine archaeological museum which has recently been extensively refurbished. Volos is also the gateway to the beautiful countryside of the Pelion with its distinctive architecture, fruit orchards and nurseries selling fragrant gardenias.

PATITIRI

On Alonnisos the majority of shops are situated in Patitiri. If you stand with your back to the port, turn right along the harbour front until you reach the Alkyon hotel on the left. Turn left here up the hill and you will pass a couple of boutiques and a creperie on your left. On the right there is an Italian ice cream parlour which sells the most amazing home-made ices and frozen yoghurts. Further on up the hill there is the National Bank of Greece and a pharmacy on the left. On the right is a ceramic/glassware shop, an internet café, shoe and clothes shops and the post office. At the top of the hill there is a greengrocer's on the left and then the 'pine tree in the road'. To the left of this is a parking area and a bakery and on the right a number of shops: 2 supermarkets, fishmonger, butcher, pharmacy, patisserie, animal food store and florist. At the top of the hill and around the bend to the left there is another greengrocer opposite the junior school and above this is the Women's co-operative of Alonnisos - Ikos - which sells a variety of traditional sweets, honey, preserves, cakes and olive oil as well as the best spanakopita (spinach pie) on the island! There is a third supermarket next to the junior school, which has a very good selection of wines. The larger supermarkets and the animal food store sell charcoal for bbq's. This is not usually on display, but if you ask for "karvouno" the owners will get you some from their store rooms. Opening times for the supermarkets are usually 08:00 – 14: 00 and 17:00 – 22:00. During high season they may open in the afternoons too. The bakery near the car park is open all day June-September and sells a variety of bread, pies, cakes and sandwiches. Gift shops usually open mid-morning, close for a siesta in the afternoon and then stay open until late into the evenings to catch those taking a post-dinner stroll!

By taking the left hand road away from the port you will find a bakery, a supermarket, several souvenir shops and shops selling beach paraphernalia (lilos, jelly sandals, buckets & spades etc.) Near the bakery is a very good jewellery shop; the owner is a goldsmith who will make or alter jewellery to your own specifications. Further along this road on the left is the 'Alonissiotissa' which sells traditional sweets, preserves and liqueurs and, just across the Marpounta road, is 'Albatross' (the newsagent and sports shop) which sells guide books, magazines, cigarettes and a good selection of snorkelling and diving equipment. On the corner of the harbour front, next to Albedo Travel, is a mini-market which is open all day during July and August.

Cigarettes and tobacco products can be purchased from this mini-market, the Kafenion next to the Alkyon hotel, the newsagents and a shop opposite the police station. The price of cigarettes is controlled by the government: both local and international brands are considerably cheaper than in the UK.

All supermarkets sell a wide range of alcoholic drinks. The quality of Greek wines has improved dramatically over the last 15 years or so, and there is a wide range of good quality wines at low prices.

Internet facilities can be found at Technokids, just past the junior school, or the internet café on the main hill near the post office. You can access Wi-Fi along Patitiri harbour front, at Technokids or the Panselinos restaurant near the bus stop in the Old Village.

There are 2 hairdressers on the island, both of whom cater to both ladies and gents. Maria has her salon opposite the post office and is there most mornings and evenings. Aneza's salon is on the right hand side of the road to Votsi harbour, a few hundred metres after you turn off the main road along the island. Aneza is there evenings only from 5-8.

VOTSI

There are 2 supermarkets on the road leading down to Votsi harbour. Off this road on the right is a butcher.

OLD VILLAGE

There are 3 mini-markets in the Old Village, 2 near the main church of Agios Nikolaos and 1 near the bus stop. All are owned by ladies called Maria who are distinguishable by age, girth, demeanour and/or location. Happy Maria and thin Maria have shops near the church of Agios Yorgos. Young(er) Maria has the bus–stop–shop which is the newest of the 3 (therefore the products on sale are less likely to have passed their sell by date and still be priced in drachmas). All the ladies sell a limited selection of fruit and vegetables. Just opposite the bus stop is a bakery and the OV branch of the Italian gelateria.

The Old Village is mainly noted for its antique and souvenir shops and it is well worth wandering through the small alleys to find interesting shops tucked away from general view. Looking across to Skopelos is café Xagiati, run by Meni who is a wonderful cook. Her cakes and pastries are a delight for those with a sweet tooth. Near the cakery is Gallery 5, which sells water-colour prints and originals and home-made candles.

STENI VALA

This is a charming fishing village with cafés/bars along the quay – just perfect for relaxing and watching people messing about in boats. There are 2 supermarkets here: Katina's and Ikaros. Both sell fresh bread, cigarettes and a limited selection of fruit and vegetables. Prices are generally higher than those in Patitiri.

NIGHT LIFE

Although Alonnisos is not as well endowed with clubs and bars as Skiathos, night owls will find some entertainment. The nice thing about bars on Alonnisos is that they are safe places for the whole family, serving not only alcoholic drinks but also coffee and ices. However, they do tend to play loud music and prices are higher than those in tavernas (but the chairs are more comfortable!).

MAP OF PATITIRI, ROUSOUM & VOTSI

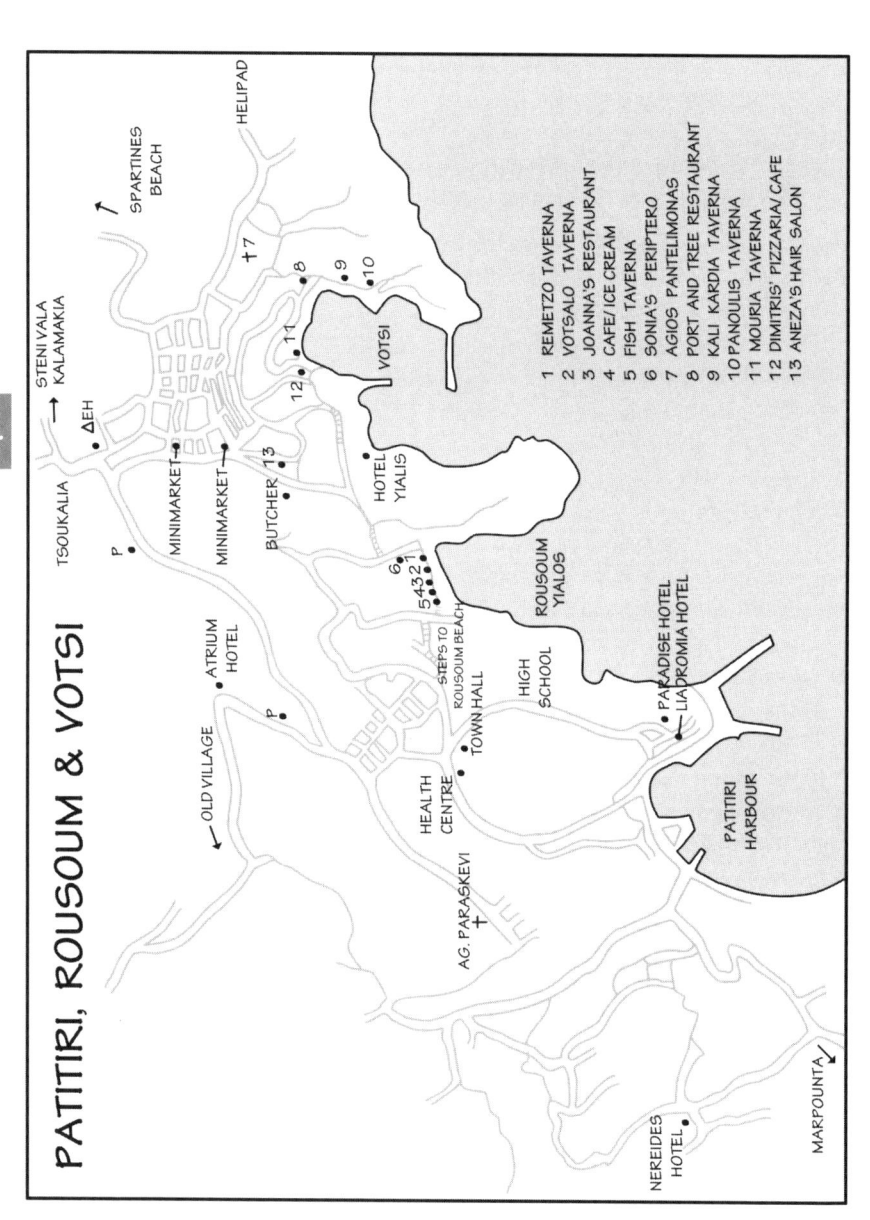

1 REMETZO TAVERNA
2 VOTSALO TAVERNA
3 JOANNA'S RESTAURANT
4 CAFE/ICE CREAM
5 FISH TAVERNA
6 SONIA'S PERIPTERO
7 AGIOS PANTELIMONAS
8 PORT AND TREE RESTAURANT
9 KALI KARDIA TAVERNA
10 PANOULIS TAVERNA
11 MOURIA TAVERNA
12 DIMITRIS' PIZZARIA/ CAFE
13 ANEZA'S HAIR SALON

MUSEUMS

Whilst on Alonnisos you might like to visit the museum of Kostas and Angela Mavrikis. If you walk along the harbour-front, with the sea on your left, take the path that runs behind the tavernas lining the back of the beach. Walk to the end of this path and then follow the steps which will lead you directly to the museum. The building itself is a tribute to Alonnisos and the islands of the marine park. The key stones over the front door are volcanic rock from Psathoura and the marble on the floors is from Skantzoura.

All the artefacts and exhibits are from the islands and have been lovingly collected over the years by the Mavrikis family. Kostas and his wife Angela have a café and shop in Steni Vala – they are extremely interesting to talk to and extremely knowledgable. Kostas has published a number of books about the history of the islands. The museum was built in 2000 and boasts a wonderful collection of implements utilised for the local occupations which have now all but vanished, an exhibit of the arms and artefacts dating from the years of piracy, and wonderful pictures, maps and objects dating from the start of the revolution in 1821 which led to the formation of an independent Greek State in 1830. In addition, the roof-top terrace and café have wonderful views over the harbour of Patitiri. In the summer months the museum is open from 11am until 7pm and the entrance fee is 4 euros.

There is also a museum in the Old Village. This is situated behind the memorial to those killed on August 15th 1944. It is designed to represent a traditional village house. This museum is run by the council, and opening times tend to vary!

MAP OF THE OLD VILLAGE

OLD VILLAGE
CHORA - PALIOCHORIO

OLD VILLAGE: CHORA, ΧΩΡΑ

1. MINIMARKET: MARIA VAFINI
2. PERI OREKSIOS: FAST FOOD
3. BAKERY
4. ITALIAN ICE CREAM
5. TAVERNA 'O NIKOS'
6. TAVERNA 'HAGIATI' (ΧΑΓΙΑΤΙ)
7. EVANGELISMOS
8. AGIOS ATHANASIOS
9. WAR MEMORIAL
10. CHURCH OF CHRIST
11. MEMORIAL TO THOSE KILLED ON 15/08/44
12. TRADITIONAL HOUSE MUSEUM
13. AGIOS NIKOLAOS
14. MINIMARKET: MARIA ANAGNOSTOU
15. MINIMARKET: MARIA MALAMATENIA
16. AGIOS YORGOS
17. TAVERNA 'KYRA NINA'
18. TAVERNA 'KASTRO'
19. GALLERY 5
20. HAGIATI: CAKES AND COFFEE
21. AGIOS DIMITRIOS
22. TAVERNA 'PARAPORT'

MAP OF BEACHES

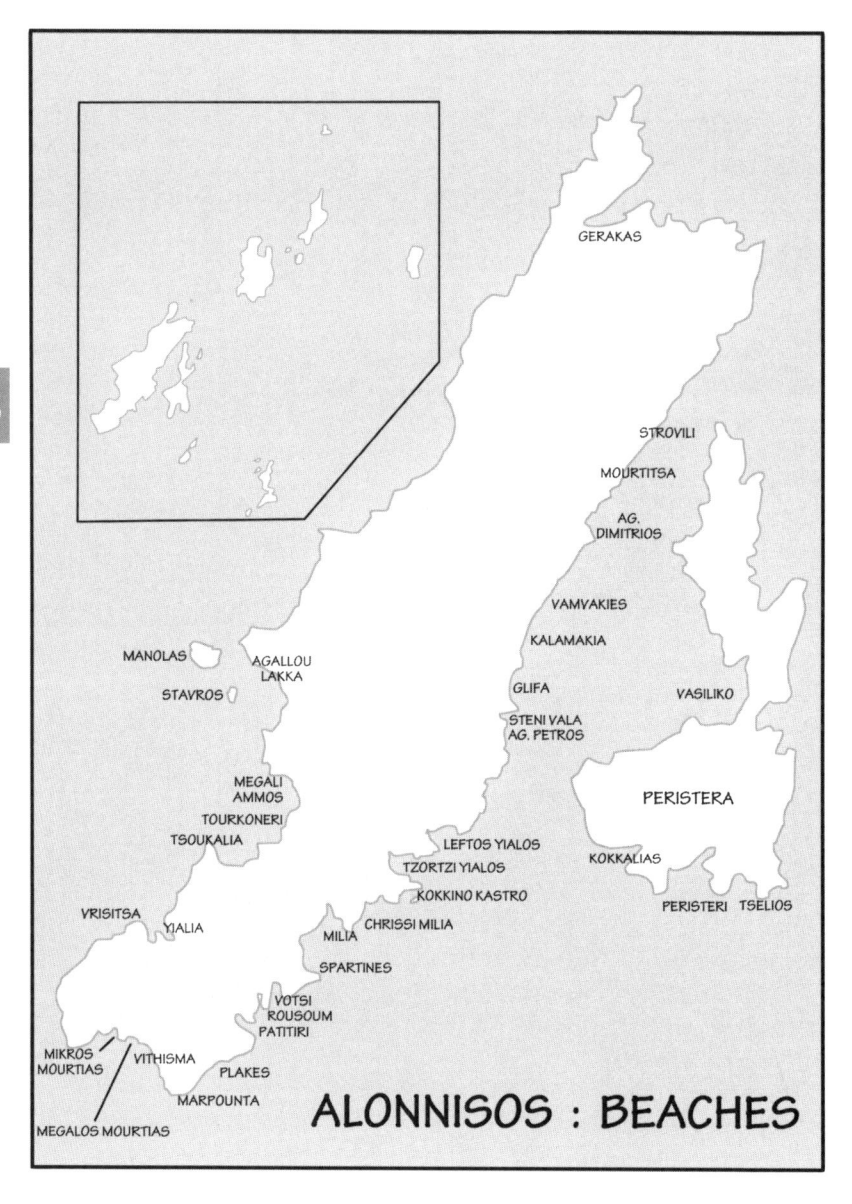

ALONNISOS : BEACHES

BEACHES

The beauty of the beaches on Alonnisos lies in the surrounding countryside and the intense clarity of the colours. Alonnisos is not blessed with sandy beaches, but neither is it cursed by overcrowding or rampant commercialism: there are no beach vendors here! There are now limited scuba diving facilities: Ikion (Steni Vala) and Poseidonas (Patitiri) will arrange trips or courses with qualified instructors and supply all necessary equipment.

Patitiri itself has a pebble beach, close to where the hydrofoils dock. Despite the proximity of this to the commercial and pleasure craft, the water is surprisingly clear. Further around the headland, past the new ferry port, there is a rocky swimming area with a ladder allowing easy immersion. **Roussoum** is a 10 minute walk from Patitiri: here there is a pebble beach and several tavernas. **Votsi** (20 minutes walk from Patitiri) also has a small beach looking out over the harbour which is home to many fishing and pleasure craft. There are tavernas on each side of the bay. Just beyond Votsi, and accessible only on foot, there is a small beach at **Spartines.**

Moving south from Patitiri, there are swimming areas to the left of the road to Marpounta. These are small inlets between the rocks which offer a certain degree of privacy, if not too much comfort - take a lilo! About 500m before Marpounta (which is an Italian Resort Hotel and closed to non-residents) there is a turning on the right which is a graded road leading to **Megalos Mourtias.** About half way along this road, high on the bank to the right, there is a memorial plaque bearing the inscription "Here Georgios Andreas Tsoumas accidentally fell and was saved by Germans in the year 1944. The Saints be praised." Just before the road

The iconostasis dedicated to Georgos Andreas Tsoumas

starts descending, and opposite a small parking area there is a track off to the left which leads to a shingle beach called **Vrithisma**. There are several ways down to the beach from the initial track but beware, the paths are quite steep and very uneven.

If you take the road from Patitiri to the Old Village, there are tracks to pebble beaches on the right hand side of the road: **Yialia** (turn right just past the turning signposted OTE) and **Vrisitsa** (turn right immediately after the corn circles). Unfortunately, as the prevailing winds blow towards this side of the island, the beaches suffer from debris, particularly plastic waste. Just before the Old Village the road to **Megalos Mourtias** bears left (and is signposted). This beach is again pebbled, but very popular. It boasts three very good tavernas, a pretty olive grove which is perfect if you need to escape the sun for a while, and beach beds and umbrellas for hire. Carrying on past the Old Village, the surfaced road gives way to a graded road which bears left and heads towards **Mikros Mourtias**. This is a quiet pebbled beach with no facilities.

As you head past Votsi towards the north of the island, the first turning on the left will lead you to **Tsoukalia**. This pebbled beach is very popular with locals, so expect it to be busier in the afternoons and at weekends. There are no tavernas or sunbeds here, only herds of goats and sheep which come to drink water from the well near the windmill. Unfortunately this beach is also exposed to the prevailing winds, so rubbish can be a problem. There is a signpost on the main road indicating that there is an archaeological site at Tsoukalia: this is a fenced-in area at the back of the beach thought to be the site of ancient kilns used to produce amphorae. Unfortunately it looks very scruffy and the pot sherds look as though they are the remains of smashed-up roofing tiles rather than ancient amphorae.

Further round the coast, on the same side of the island, is the bay of **Megali Ammos**. This means 'big sand' in Greek, but unfortunately the majority of the sand is under the sea and the beach is again mostly pebbles. The bay is divided into small, separate beaches such as **Tourkoneri**: they have no facilities but are very quiet and absolutely beautiful. The bay is sheltered from the northerly winds, so the beaches are much cleaner than those nearer Patitiri. Coming up a little from the coast, the main graded road continues north-west, through a large gate with the start of walking path 7 on the right and the path to Makris Kavos on the left. The gate is for the benefit of the goats and sheep, so please close it behind you. After another 2 km of winding, progressively worsening, road you will be at **Agallou Lakka,** where you will find a very small beach and no more road. This is as far as it is possible to drive on the northwestern side of the island: well worth the effort if only to see the changing vegetation and the dramatic scenery, especially that looking back towards Skopelos and the islets of Agios Yorgos.

The beaches on the relatively sheltered southeast side of the island are more popular and therefore more populous. Taking the main road to the north of the island, the turning to **Milia** is about 2 km past Votsi. The pebbled beach is set in a stunning bay surrounded by mature pine forest. The summer of 2008 saw the surprising introduction of a marine bouncy castle here – unfortunately repeated in 2009. **Chrissi Milia** is the next turning off the main road - this is the only sandy beach on the island. The sea is very shallow and therefore ideal for small children. The taverna overlooking the beach is very good, beds & brollies are available. The down side to Chrissi Milia is that, because of the sand and the proximity of a fairly large resort hotel, the beach can get fairly crowded (this is relative, compared to Brighton on a bank holiday it is positively deserted).

Travelling northwards, there are beaches at **Kokkinokastro** (a small area of sand at one end, pebbles at the other), **Tzortzi Gialos** (pebbles, one taverna open only at peak season), **Leftos Yialos** (pebbles, two excellent tavernas, sunbeds and brollies), **Agios Petros** (pebbles) and on to **Steni Vala** (shops, cafes, tavernas and more pebbles). At the back of the beach at Steni Vala is the Monk Seal Rehabilitation Unit. Just over the headland from Steni Vala there is **Glyfa**. This is a pretty beach (pebbles & sunbeds) looking towards the island of Peristera.

The road proceeds along the coast through **Kalamakia** (a small harbour with several tavernas, all serving excellent fresh seafood) and **Vamvakies** and terminates at **Agios Dimitrios.** This is a triangular spit of land jutting into the sea. The beach is a comfortable shingle. There is a small kantina serving snack and drinks and a very traditional taverna serving excellent cheese pies. Beach beds and brollies are available for hire. However, the beach at Agios Dimitrios is large and the north-facing part of the beach is much quieter.

There are, of course, other beaches which are less easy to get to and have fewer facilities. Part of the fun of Alonnisos is finding these and having them all to yourselves!

Plakes beach

The Old Village Alonia (corn circles)

A BRIEF HISTORY OF ALONNISOS

Alonnisos has had its share of invaders and occupants throughout the years. Before the 8th century BC, a tribe called the Dolopes inhabited the island. The main street in Patitiri is named Odos Ikion Dolopes after this tribe. In 478 BC Alonnisos (at this time known as Ikos) was part of the Athenian Alliance before being captured by the Spartans in 403 BC and subsequently retaken by the Athenians. The island prospered under the influence of Philip of Macedon but fell to the Romans in 146 BC. This sovereignty lasted until the fall of the Roman Empire: one major influence of this period was the introduction of Christianity. The islands then became part of the Byzantine Empire and at this time Alonnisos was known as Chiliodromia.

The oldest part of the Old Village has a Byzantine fortress construction. The walls of the fortress consisted of the face of the rock on one side and the outside walls of the houses on the other. The main gate to the citadel was called 'Portara', the original key to which is still kept in the council offices. There was also a smaller door (the Paraporta) which acted as an escape route. During the Ottoman rule the average family consisted of 6 people who shared a small house of about 40 square metres.

When the Ottomans broke up the Byzantine Empire in 1453, Alonnisos came under Venetian control. The last person to loot the Old Village was the infamous Barbarossa (Red Beard) in 1538. Khair-el-din Barbarossa and his brother Horuk (beheaded in 1518) were renegade Greeks, natives of Mytilene. Khair-el-din acted as an admiral to the Ottoman ruler Suleiman I during a period of extraordinary Turkish expansionism. Belgrade was taken in 1521 (the rest of Serbia was in Turkish hands by 1459) and the Hungarian army was slaughtered at Mohacs in 1526. In 1522 Suleiman sent a huge fleet to Rhodes to oust the Knights of St. John who, by then, had turned to piracy. By 1529 the Ottoman armies were pressing at the gates of Vienna. Barbarossa died in 1546 in Constantinople. The Venetians lost their influence in the Northern Sporades in 1537/38 and Turkish rule was introduced.

The revolution of 1821 against Turkish rule led to the subsequent establishment of the Hellenic State under the Treaty of London in 1830. In 1821 the population of Alonnisos (at this time called Iliodromia) was said to be around 300. When in 1822 the Greek National Congress met in Epidavros, the Dimos (community) of Alonnisos was founded, although the islands were actually governed by a Vice-Administrator called Pavlos Sideris. Despite freedom from Turkish rule the islands were still badly plagued by pirates and, in addition, had to pay heavy revenues to the new government to cover the cost of the revolution. Times were very hard!

Between 1834 and 1837 the government of Greece, with King Otto of Bavaria at its head, sent a mining expert (Dr Karl Gustav Fiedler) to survey the kingdom for mineral resources. When he came to Alonnisos he discovered 11 graves (mnimata) near Kokkinokastro, 2 of which were intact. On opening the graves he found that they had a storage space near the feet of the skeletons for those items accompanying the dead. Each of these spaces held at least one amphora, one oil jar, a lamp and several drinking vessels. All the bodies were laid with their heads pointing south. In addition, the graves were lined with limestone and near the head and feet a limestone plate was used to limit the space. Fiedler obtained permission to take the artifacts with him but unfortunately they were damaged en route. He also took samples of lignite with him, but one can only assume that the island was not found to be rich in minerals.

In 1836 the island was named Alonnisos. This name is derived from 'Alon' (the ancient Greek word for salt) and 'Nisos' (island). Before this date, documents mentioning the island of 'Alonnisos' were actually referring as the island now known as Kyra Panagia. In 1848, a census gave the population of Alonnisos as 312. This rose to 498 in 1889 and to 653 in 1896.

The wine press in Patitiri

In 1912/13 Alonnisos lost 7 men in the Balkan Wars and they are commemorated on a memorial in the Plateia in the Old Village. A further 2 names were added to the memorial in 1920/22, islanders who lost their lives in the Graeco-Turkish war which culminated in the Turkish occupation of the Greek enclave of Smyrna and the massacre of approximately 30,000 of its Greek and Armenian citizens. In 1916 the first house was built in Patitiri (which takes its name from the wine presses which were situated there: 'paton' – he who treads or presses) by Yiannis Christos, much to the bemusement of the people in the Old Village, who thought him crazy!

During the WWII there was no permanent German garrison on Alonnisos but there were regular inspections by German soldiers from Thessaloniki, which was the Aegean HQ of the German army. On August 15th 1944, 10 islanders were gathered for execution in the Old Village. Nine of these were killed but the tenth, Apostolis Vlaikos, survived. Popular lore has it that, just as the execution was about to take place, someone shouted to say that his wife had just given birth to a son: the German officer missed him (whether by accident or design) and he survived, albeit with a hearing problem as the bullet hit the wall near his ear. This same Apostolis Vlaikos was elected Mayor in the 1970's. There is a separate memorial to the nine men who were killed near the entrance to the Kastro: the original plaque was unveiled on 15th August 1984 and the inscription read 'To the patriots who gave their lives for our freedom, executed by the Germans on August 15th 1944'. This was replaced with another plaque on 15th August 1999. Part of the new inscription was taken from a poem by Cavafy – The Thermopylae – and reads "Honour to those who waged their lives to defend the Thermopylae and never forgetting this vow. To the honour of those patriots executed by the Germans of the third Reich, giving their lives for our liberty 15.8.1944".

The Greek civil war was a particularly bloody episode in the nation's history: in addition to the atrocities carried out by both sides, the country did not use the post-war period to work toward producing a sound economic base in order to improve the standard of living. In fact, all foreign aid and available wealth went toward the suppression of communism. No communist or partisan groups were permanently housed on Alonnisos, but another 3 names were added to the memorial in 1948 and from time to time partisan boats landed on the island to take supplies of livestock.

At the beginning of the 1950's Alonnisos was a producer of very fine wine: in 1950 the harvest yielded 257,530 litres. Within 3 years the production fell to zero as the vines were decimated by Phylloxera.

In 1961 the first non-Greeks came to the island to build sea-side houses. In 1962 an Athenian, Manos Kalogridis, opened the first tourist accommodation on Alonnisos – the Artemis Bungalows, which can still be seen above Patitiri on the Marpounta road.

By the mid-1960's the harbour in Patitiri came into use. Up until this time a caique went every morning from Mikros Mourtias to Skopelos, returning in the evening. Also at this time Christos Athanassiou wrote an article about the island. This man, nicknamed 'O Sophos' (the wise man), worked as a counsellor and healer at a time when there was no doctor on the island. His son, Yorgos, is now the senior doctor at the Health Centre on Alonnisos. The wise man died on March 3rd 1988 at the age of 76. The main crops on the island were olives, cereals, almonds and citrus fruit, but nearly 40% of the per capita income was provided by remittances from family members working either on the mainland or abroad. The income for islanders at this time was only about 54% of the national average income in Greece.

On March 9th 1965 an earthquake shook Alonnisos and the surrounding islands. Aerial photographs taken shortly after the earthquake showed that about 110 houses had been damaged to some extent. Frederika, the Queen Mother (wife of the recently deceased King Paul and mother of the newly crowned King Constantine II) visited the islands affected by the 'quake – her helicopter landed behind the cemetery on Alonnisos. Military personnel also came to the island and built a simple road from the harbour in Patitiri to the Old Village. The government promised new houses in Patitiri for those whose houses were damaged.

December 1965 was an important month for Alonnisos – it saw the arrival of Father Gregory as the island's priest. Father Gregory, or 'Papouli' as he is affectionately known, is still here and has been a source of inspiration to the

Kastro, the Old Village

inhabitants, Orthodox and non-Orthodox alike. He has now retired and Father Avram has taken his place as island priest.

In 1966 the church of Agios Nikolaos in the Old Village was rebuilt and the following year saw the construction of a primary school in Patitiri. Unfortunately 1967 also saw a military coup in Athens designed to pre-empt a Centre Union victory at the polls, which heralded the start of 7 years of military dictatorship. In 1968 construction of the new settlement in Patitiri was started and this was finished 2 years later. During this time a power station was built in Votsi which provided Patitiri and Votsi with electricity. Power was not taken up to the Old Village until 1987.

The 231 'pre-fabs' (concrete rectangles built for those evacuated from the Old Village) were ready for occupation in 1970 but these were quite primitive and had no drinking-water or sewage systems. The evacuation of the Old Village was not achieved en masse but over the course of several years. The last evacuees only made the move in 1977 after the water supply to the Old Village was cut off and the school was closed.

The construction of a new church in Patitiri – Agia Paraskevi – was started in 1970 on the site of the old one which had been damaged by the earthquake. This new church was consecrated in 1977.

Meanwhile, more foreigners and mainland Greeks were buying houses on the island. In 1971 the airport on Skiathos was opened. In 1974 extensions to the harbour were started to allow larger vessels to dock. At this time there was only 1 car on the island – the priest's – and a couple of trucks. A dirt road was built between Patitiri and Votsi. In July 1974 the Military Junta of the 'Colonels' was deposed and Greece returned to civilian rule.

By 1976 only a few families and their livestock lived in the Old Village. Conversely, the Paraport taverna was opened and the following year Maria Anagnostou opened a 'pantopoleion' (literally, a shop which sells everything) in the Old Village. The Alonia, the 5 'corn' or threshing circles near the village, were still used. A mule was tethered to a central pole and pulled a 'dokani'. This was a heavy plank studded with flint-like stones. As the stones were drawn over the wheat they separated the grain from the chaff. The tether shortened as the mule walked around the central pole and so the dokani was drawn over the entire circle. If you stand at the circles on a clear day and look out directly over the small islet of Manolas in the bay of Megali Ammos you can see Mount Athos.

Meanwhile construction was continuing in Patitiri, not only for the enforced relocation from the Old Village but also to fulfil the dowry custom whereby daughters are given a house of their own when they get married. In 1978 the Fisherman's cooperative was established by Pakis Athanassiou. In 1980 Alonnisos got its first taxi.

On January 1st 1981 Greece became a member of the EEC. This has led to many changes in the island's infrastructure as funds have become available, giving the island the helipad, surfaced roads, harbour extensions etc. 1982 saw the opening of the 'Aloni' taverna in the Old Village by Panagiotis Kalogiannis (alas, he is no longer with us but the taverna is now run by his daughter and her husband) and the first bus between Patitiri and the Old Village (a one-way fare being 100 drachmae). The next year Alonnisos got its first pharmacy, the rubbish dump was moved from behind the cemetery to the west of Kalovolos and the 'dimos' got its first rubbish truck. In the summer of the following year the second of the Marias (Maria Malamatenia) opened her pantopoleion – 5 steps away from her competitor's shop – and a memorial plaque was unveiled commemorating the deaths of the 9 men killed by the Germans in 1944.

In 1985 the first summer rubbish collection was made in the Old Village by Mitso and his mule, testament to the fact that this area was gradually being repopulated. Also, traffic between the islands was greatly enhanced by the service offered by the flying dolphins. The following year preliminary plans were formulated for the creation of the National Marine Park of Alonnisos, Northern Sporades (NMPANS), although this was not officially ratified until the presidential decree was signed in 1992. Also in this year the Biological Research Station at Gerakas was opened by the Aga Khan, whose Bellerive Foundation funded its construction. The MoM society currently has information centres in Patitiri and at Gerakas (sadly, to date no research has been carried out at the research station) and a rehabilitation unit on the beach at Steni Vala.

During the last 15 years of the 20th century there were many changes on the island. A lane was made linking Megalos Mourtias with the Old Village. The previously abandoned settlement at Mourtero was 'rediscovered'. Mourtero had a population of about 60 people at the beginning of the 20th century but after the second world war the settlement was gradually abandoned, with the inhabitants moving to Patitiri. 1987 saw the beginning of construction of the houses in the lower part of the Old Village: the following year graves were found on this site but, although the authorities were notified, the archaeological service carried out no excavations. Also in 1988 the 'Hellenic Society for the protection of the Mediterranean Monk Seal' was set up. In 1989 the first part of the road from Patitiri to the Old Village was surfaced.

In 1990 the rubbish tip was moved yet again, to the old quarry near the OTE towers. More tarmac was laid on the road to the Old Village, this time as far as the OTE (the state telecommunications company) turning. It wasn't until 2 years later that the tarmac stretched all the way from Patitiri to the Old Village.

In June 1992 government marine archaeologists investigated a wreck found in deep water off the southern end of Peristera. The investigation indicated that the ship dated from 400BC and was considerably larger than ships of that time were thought to be: it contained 4000 amphorae. The huts built on Peristera for the divers and their equipment can still be seen. In August of the same year an enormous forest fire engulfed the areas around Chrissi Milia, Kokkinokastro and Tzortzi Gialos.

1992 also saw construction of the helipad in Votsi and the decommissioning of the electrical generation plant: electricity now reached the island from the mainland via undersea cables. In 1994/5 the offices of the state electricity company, DEH, were erected on the site of the defunct power station.

Other important additions to the island were built in 1992: the medical centre in Patitiri and the secondary school. Construction of the school, comprising a gymnasium and lyceum (junior and senior high schools), was funded by Konstantinos Kalogiannis, an islander who had emigrated to the USA as a child. Previously, children had had to travel to Skopelos daily or move to the mainland to continue their education past primary level. Every May the children hold a cultural and sporting festival called Kalogianneia, with the participation of children from Skopelos and Skiathos, to honour their benefactor.

By the summer of 1994 several public telephones had sprung up in the Old Village and Patitiri. A new memorial was erected near the Town Hall, this one bearing a quotation from Thucydides "The whole world is the grave of famous men". The state telecommunications company (OTE) built an office next to the health centre: not of great use, as the inhabitants still have to go to the office on Skopelos if they have any problems with the phone lines. However, in the autumn of 1996 OTE laid new fibre-optic cables which enabled many more households to get telephone lines (up to this point someone had to die before you could get a phone connection), so they have atoned in part for the white elephant of the office.

1995 saw the opening of the National Bank in Patitiri (previously the nearest bank (Emporiki – Commercial) was on Skopelos, with a couple of tourist offices in Patitiri running local franchises). Restoration work was started on the old chapel at Agii Anargiroi. On May 1st the International Academy of Homeopathy was inaugurated and the following year hosted a symposium on archaeological research in the Northern Sporades.

In 1996 Alonnisos became an autonomous community within the regional administrative district of Magnesia. The foundation stone for the new Town Hall was laid by the mayor Yiannis Drossakis on May 15th. All the time more roads were being made and/or surfaced, more phone boxes were being installed, and lanes and pavements in Patiriri and the Old Village were tiled with Pelion slate (called plaka). In the summer of 1997 the roads were embellished with white lines! During the following year another pharmacy opened and the donkey path (calderimi) between Patitiri and the Old Village was restored, paved and lit. On 11th October 1998, local elections voted in a new mayor, Orestes Papachristou (PASOK) but it was the outgoing mayor who inaugurated the new Town Hall on December 27th of the same year.

In 1999 the community, funded by the EU, cleared, mapped and waymarked 14 hiking trails. The port area of Patitiri was given a face lift: flowers were planted along the cliff under the Kavos area, a special imprinted surface was laid over the port, lights were installed under the cliffs on the Marpounta side of the harbour and waste bins were dotted around. The council also instigated a beach-cleaning programme, although this seems to have become a little haphazard. In June of this year, the Department of Archaeology of the University of Nebraska carried out preparatory work on the excavation of the kilns at Tsoukalia and a fence was erected to secure the site. Sign posts to the site have been erected, but usually the visitor is somewhat disappointed at how little there is to see. Work was also carried out on the site of a Byzantine basilica at Agios Dimitrios, but similarly there is little to see.

Since the turn of the century work has continued to surface the roads and install a more reliable electrical system. The water supply has improved immeasurably. Wells at Mega Nero (big water) were the main source of water for the island until 1993 but now water for the majority of village houses is piped from wells and catchments in the north of the island. Water being supplied at present has been shown to come from an aquifer on the Pelion via underwater channels. Houses outside village limits are still dependent on collecting rainwater during the winter and storing this in large cisternas under their terraces.

The island is greatly dependent on ferries for all the produce imported: these days dairy products and fruit & vegetables are brought over on trucks from the mainland whereas previously everything was brought to the island on a weekly caique. The relatively small ferries that serviced Alonnisos were very slow and inefficient with respect to the available garage space. Now the island is visited by much larger, quicker ferries (although not as often!): to enable these to dock safely a new ferry port had to be constructed. Unfortunately this is not quite finished and the lack of an extensive sea wall means that if the seas are running from the south it is very difficult for the ferries to dock.

On January 1st 2001, Greece switched currencies from the drachma to the euro: even on such a small island the transition was effected without fuss or too many headaches although, strangely enough, people still seem to refer to land prices in drachmae!

Since the turn of the century there have continued to be changes to the island. More roads have been surfaced, such as those to Tsoukalia, Leftos Yialos, Kato Chorafi and the old road to Vamvakies from the Gerakas road. Our mayor, Orestes Papachristou, was replaced by Panagiotis Vlaikos at the last local elections. Currently a reservoir is under construction at the start of the Kastana George at Diassolo. The number of cars on the island has increased dramatically so that parking is becoming a big problem at the height of the season. Even more alleys and lanes in the Old Village have been plaka'd. The building industry has taken a bit of a nose-dive of late: the increase in the cost of building materials and the increased cost of fuel used in getting them to the island has pushed construction costs very high. And of course, recession has hit Greece just as it has everywhere else in Europe: the islands now rely on tourism as their main source of income, so the economic woes are felt strongly here.

In 2009 there was a change of government in Greece: Konstantinos Karamanlis (Nea Democratia) called a snap election for October of this year and was soundly beaten at the polls by Georgios Papandreaou's PASOK party. Let's see what benefit this brings to Alonnisos!

THE GREEK ALPHABET

α	Α	άλφα	alpha	alpha
β	Β	βήτα	beta	veeta
γ	Γ	γάμα	gamma	gamma
δ	Δ	δέλτα	delta	thelta
ε	Ε	έψιλον	epsilon	epsilon
ζ	Ζ	ζήτα	zeta	zeeta
η	Η	ήτα	eta	eeta
θ	Θ	θήτα	theta	theta
ι	Ι	γιώτα	iota	eeota
κ	Κ	κάπα	kappa	kappa
λ	Λ	λάμδα	lambda	lambtha
μ	Μ	μι	mu	mee
ν	Ν	νι	nu	nee
ξ	Ξ	ξι	xi	ksee
ο	Ο	όμικρον	omicron	omicron
π	Π	πι	pi	pea
ρ	Ρ	ρο	rho	row
σ	Σ	σίγμα	sigma	sigma
τ	Τ	ταυ	tau	taf
υ	Υ	ύψιλον	upsilon	eepsilon
φ	Φ	φι	phi	phee
χ	Χ	χι	chi	kee
ψ	Ψ	ψι	psi	psee
ω	Ω	ωμέγα	omega	omega

Combinations of letters also produce distinctive sounds:

ου	oo	as in p**oo**l	γγ	ng	as in ha**ng**
αι	e	as in b**e**t	γκ	g	as in **g**as
ει	ee	as in b**ee**t	τζ	j	as in **j**ewel
οι	ee	as in b**ee**t	μπ	b	as in **b**all
αυ	af or av		ντ	d	as in **d**oor
ευ	ef or ev		γχ	nch	as in mela**nch**oly

MIND YOUR LANGUAGE

Here are a few words of Greek to help you in tavernas and shops: the local people are generally pleased when visitors make the effort to speak in their language, but they will probably answer you in English. Given the speed at which they speak, that is probably just as well!

Hello and/or goodbye	γεια σου	yassou (pl. yassas: used when addressing more than one person or when being formal, such as when speaking to an elderly person)
Good morning	κάλη μέρα	kali mera
Good evening	κάλη σπέρα	kali spera
Good night	κάλη νίχτα	kali nikta
Yes/no	ναι/όχι	nai/ochi
Thank you	ευχαριστώ	efcharisto
Please/you are welcome	παρακαλώ	parakalo
Good	καλά	kala
How much...	πόσο κάνει	poso kani
Very expensive	πόλυ ακριβό	poli akrivo
What time is it	τι ώρα είναι	ti ora inay
Where is...	που είναι	pou inay
OK	εντάξει	endaxi
I want/would like	θέλω/θα ήθελα	thelo/tha eethela
Large/small	μεγάλο/μικρό	megalo/mikro
1,2,3	ένα, δυο, τρία	ena, thio, tria
Half	μισό	miso
I don't understand	θεν καταλαβαίνω	then katalaveno
Excuse me/sorry	συγγνώμη	signomi
Open/closed	ανοικτό/κλειστό	aneekto/kleisto
Right/left	δεξιά/αριστερά	thexia/aristera
Till, cash desk	ταμείο	tameio
Bill	λογαριασμός	logariasmos
Can I....	μπορώ να	boro na
I am a vegetarian	είμαι χορτοφάγος	eemay hortofagos

FESTIVALS & CELEBRATIONS

Many of the festivals and celebrations have a religious basis, so are observed in accordance with the Orthodox calendar. Over 95% of the population of Greece is Orthodox: indeed, it is said that being Orthodox and speaking Greek are the two most important criteria in defining a Greek, irrespective of birthplace. The religion has changed little since the founding of the church by Constantine in the 4th century. This constancy can perhaps explain the violence of Iconoclasm, a movement which sought to change the rules. In the early 8th century, the Byzantine emperor Leo III deemed that images of divine beings were sacrilegious. Iconoclasm began the rift with Rome which was exacerbated in 800 when the Pope crowned Charlemagne as emperor, so usurping the authority of the Emperor of Constantinople. Further divisions arose over the celibacy of the clergy, and the use of the phrase "and the son" in the Holy Creed. The final 'schism' came about in 1054 when the Pope's representative, Cardinal Humbert, excommunicated the Patriarch of Constantinople, Michael Cerularius.

In Greece, the church permeates every layer of life. If you have a problem, it is customary to light a candle to the saint most likely to hear your prayers. You may also buy the protection of an icon - a small, flat metal image representing the object of your concern. Icons of ships, houses, crops, men, women, babies and various anatomical parts can be seen in all churches. During the 400 years of Turkish oppression, it was the Church which gave the people their unity and preserved a sense of national identity. The churches and monasteries were

Icons in the church of Ag. Yorgos

also the custodians of the music, art, literature and spoken history that survive today.

When Christianity supplanted the polytheistic religions of pagan Greece, elements of the old religions were incorporated with those of the new. Although the last pagan temples were closed in 392 AD, the special protections that the old gods offered could be transferred to a particular Christian saint. Like the old gods, today's saints are often revered at shrines and tiny chapels which are generally built to give thanks. There are literally thousands of them, housing an icon with an oil lamp and a never-ending supply of olive oil in assorted containers. Devout travellers will fuel the lamps, tend the wicks and perhaps leave some coins for its upkeep in the box provided. Shrines to pagan gods were built in the same locations and for the same reasons: to provide travellers with a moment of rest and a chance to reflect before resuming their journey.

Births & Baptisms

Traditionally, a woman is not allowed to leave the house (or have a shower!) for 40 days after the birth of her baby. At the baptism, the naked child is immersed 3 times in Holy water to renounce the devil and a small lock of hair is cut from the baby's head. After immersion, female relatives dress the child in a new outfit bought by the god-parents: this symbolises the fact that the child is starting life afresh as a member of the church. For extra protection from the forces of evil, the child is given a filakto, the 'blue eye'. It is customary to name the child after one of its grandparents.

Weddings

The announcement of an engagement is often as big a cause for celebration as the wedding itself, and really marks the formal beginning of the couple's life together. On the wedding day, the best man (koumbaros) leads a procession of musicians to the groom's house to escort him and his family to the church, after being given wine and sweets. From the groom's house the procession goes to the bride's house to lead them to the church too. Once at the church the ceremony is marked by the placing of white crowns, bound together by a white ribbon, on the heads of the bride and groom. The best man then exchanges these back and forth. The newlyweds are then led around the altar 3 times and the guests shower the couple with rice (to symbolise fertility) and flower petals. Wedding guests are traditionally given a small boboniera of candied almonds: the slightly bitter taste of the almond and the sweetness of the coating symbolise the bitter-sweet nature of the couple's life together. From the church, the whole congregation goes to the reception for feasting (the traditional wedding food is goat cooked with spaghetti) and dancing, particularly the 'Syrtaki'. The father of the bride traditionally leads the dance to being with and then the groom takes over, symbolising the fact that the father has given his daughter to her new husband. The couple is provided with a fully equipped house by the bride's parents, and usually one room will have been made ready for the first child.

Funerals

These take place, because of climate, as soon after death as possible. The cemetery on Alonnisos is next to the church of the Panagia in the Old Village. This is beautifully kept, and if you pass by at dusk you will see the twinkling lights from the candles on each grave. The dead are buried with their heads pointing east: this is so that they will be able to witness the angel's trumpet blasts to signal the second coming of Christ. Memorials for the dead take place 3, 9 and 40 days after death: sweet buns and sugared wheat and raisin kouliva are given out after the ceremonies. Widows traditionally wear black for at least 3 years after the death of their husbands, but more frequently they wear black for the rest of their lives. After a period of time (not less than 3 years) the body is exhumed, washed with rose water and certain bones (particularly the skull and thigh bones) are placed in a casket in the ossuary or taken to the family's land.

Carnival (Apokriatika)

The pre-lenten carnival season lasts for 3 weeks, and climaxes during the 7th weekend before Easter. Children dress up and roam the streets and cafes where they are given sweets and money. The carnival procession has now become an institution throughout Greece and Alonnisos is no exception. The parade leaves from the council offices and threads its way through Patitiri and then on to Votsi. The council generously provides bottles of whisky to keep the spirit alive and the chill spring winds out, and people whose houses line the route appear with plates of pies and other home-made delicacies for those taking part: and here that is pretty much everybody! Loud-speakers blast out music all afternoon and there is much dancing and 'kefi,' well into the evening.

Clean Monday (Kathara Deftera)

The day after the excesses of carnival comes the start of Lent. This day is so called as it was the day on which Greek housewives cleaned all their kitchen utensils to get rid of the last traces of carnival food. Traditionally, people head for the mountains or sea shores and eat salads and sea food, especially sea urchins. There is special bread baked on clean Monday - lagana - which is long and flat, with rounded corners and lots of sesame seeds. It is traditional for children to fly kites on Clean Monday.

Easter (Paska)

This is by far the most important festival in the Orthodox year. Easter begins on the Saturday of Lazarus (the day before Palm Sunday) when children sing the hymn of Lazarus and collect money and eggs. On the morning of Palm Sunday people gather in church and are given a cross made of palm fronds which they keep for the whole of the coming year. Throughout Holy Week there are services at the church. On Thursday children dye their eggs red, to symbolise the blood of Christ. After the reading of the 12th gospel at the evening service, the ladies decorate the bier (Epitafios) so that on Good Friday morning it is ready to receive the image of the body of Christ when He is taken down from the cross.

Good Friday is a day of mourning. Shops and businesses are closed and flags are flown at half-mast. Sweet things are not eaten for the love of Christ, who was given only vinegar to drink. Soup made with sesame paste, lettuce, or lentils with vinegar are the only things eaten. It is considered a sin to work with a hammer and nails, or to sew, on Good Friday. The first great public ceremony takes place on Good Friday evening as the descent from the cross is lamented in church. The Epitafios is paraded solemnly through the streets. Everyone carries a lighted candle as they follow the bier, the priest, the cantors and the altar boys.

On the evening of Holy Saturday the resurrection mass (Anastasis) takes place. At the stroke of midnight the lights in the church are extinguished, to symbolise the darkness which enveloped Christ as He passed through the underworld. Then the priest appears from behind the iconostasis with a lighted taper, chanting "this is the light of the world". The priest lights the candles of those members of the congregation nearest him, and they then light the candles of their neighbours. This continues throughout the church until the whole congregation, both inside the church and in the courtyard, is holding lighted candles. Fireworks explode all around and people greet each other with Christos Anesti (Christ is risen) and the response Alithos Anesti (truly, He is risen).

Worshippers then take the lighted candles home with them - it is considered to bring good luck to the house if the candles are still alight when you get home. A sign of the cross is made with the flame on the lintel of the door, leaving a black smudge visible for the rest of the year.

The fast is then broken with mageiritsa, a soup made from eggs, rice and lamb offal. On Easter Sunday lamb or goat is roasted on spits, the wine flows and celebrations continue all day. Children 'knock' their dyed eggs, and the owner of the last uncracked egg is considered lucky. There is a special sweet bread, tsourekia, which is plaited and into which a red egg is baked.

Caper plant

SAINTS' DAYS

Saints' days are also celebrated as name days. It is customary to wish people Chronia Polla (many years, the equivalent of many happy returns). Most days of the year celebrate one saint or another, so the chances are that on any given day there is a festival somewhere! If the shop keepers and taverna owners are celebrating their name day, it is customary for them to offer their visitors a small cake or sweet.

January 1st (Protochronia). This is the feast day of Agios Vassilis and is celebrated with church services and the baking of a special loaf (vassilopita) into which a coin is baked. Finding the coin brings good luck for the year.

January 6th (Epiphany, Agia Theofania, Fota). This is the day on which the hobgoblins, which run riot on earth for the 12 days of Christmas, are re-banished to the underworld by various rites of the Church. The most important of these is the blessing of baptismal fonts and all outdoor bodies of water. At lakeside, seaside or riverside locations the priest casts a crucifix into the water and local youths compete to retrieve it.

Local children jumping into the harbour on January 6th, to recover the crucifix

January 7th Agios Yiannis
January 30th Holy Trinity
March 25th Independence Day and the feast of the Annunciation (Evangelismos). This is both a religious and a national holiday. There are military parades and dancing to celebrate the beginning of the revolt against Turkish rule in 1821, and church services to honour the news given to Mary that she was to become the Mother of Christ.

April 23rd Agios Yorgos (St. George), the patron of shepherds. If April 23rd falls during lent, the festivities are postponed until the Monday after Easter.

May 1st This is the day on which townspeople traditionally head for the countryside to picnic. Wreaths are hung on doorways and balconies until they are burned on bonfires on St. John's Eve (June 23rd): June 24th marks the birth of St. John the Baptist.

May 21st The feast of Agios Konstantinos and his mother Agia Eleni, the first pro-Orthodox Byzantine rulers.

May/June Analipsis, Ascension Day, celebrated 40 days after Easter

May/June Celebrated 50 days after Easter, the Monday of Agios Pnevma (the Holy Spirit) marks the appearance of this to the disciples.

June 29th The feast of Agios Petros and Agios Pavlos (St. Peter and St. Paul).

July 17th The feast of Agia Marina, the protector of crops.

July 20th The feast of Profitis Ilias (the Prophet Elijah) is widely celebrated at the hill-top shrines dedicated to him.

July 26th Agia Paraskevi. She is the Patron Saint of the main church in Patitiri and her day is marked with a procession around the town.

August 6th Metamorfosis tou Sotiros, the Transfiguration of the Saviour.

August 15th Apokimisis tis Panagia, the Assumption of the Blessed Virgin Mary. Most Greeks return to their home villages for this celebration. On Alonnisos the festival is celebrated at the Church of the Panagia in the Old Village, and there is food, wine and dancing all night.

August 23rd Genesis tis Panagia, the Birth of the Virgin Mary. This is celebrated at the church of the Panagia at Vouno.

August 29th Apokefalisis tou Prodhromou, the beheading of St. John the Baptist

September 14th Ipsosis tou Stavrou, the Exaltation of the Cross.

September 24th The feast of Agios Ioannis Theologos, St. John the Divine.

October 26th The feast of Agios Dimitrios.

October 28th Ochi Day. This is a national holiday marked by parades, speeches and dancing to commemorate the reply given to Mussolini's 1940 ultimatum about Italian occupation of Greece, by the then Prime Minister, Colonel Ioannis Metaxas: "Ochi" (No!).

November 8th The feast of the Archangels Michael and Gabriel (ton Taxiarhon).

December 6th The feast of Agios Nikolaos, the patron of seafarers.

December 25th Christouyenna, Christmas.

December 26th Synaxis tis Panagia, the Meeting of the Virgin's Entourage.

December 27th Agios Stephanos

CHURCHES ON ALONNISOS

1. Agios Athanassios: situated in the Plateia of the Old Village, near the war memorial. This is one of the oldest churches on Alonnisos
2. Agios Yorgos: this is a vaulted basilica built at the highest point of the Old Village and dating from the 17th century.
3. Agios Nikolaos: situated in the Kastro of the Old Village. The original church was demolished in 1964 and replaced by the newer version that is there at present.
4. Agios Dimitrios: destroyed by the earthquake, the ruins lie in the southern part of the Old Village
5. Evangelismos: this is a basilica with a vaulted roof and dates from the 17th - 18th century. It is situated near the well in the Old Village.
6. Church of Christ: situated on the northern side of the Old Village this dates from the 17th century. The entrance at the western side leads into a small narthex and a gallery for women.
7. Church of the Panagia: this is adjacent to the cemetery, just past the Old Village. It is the site for the services to mark the Assumption of the Virgin Mary on August 15th.
8. Agios Yiannis: if you take the main road from the Old Village towards Patitiri, you will see the threshing circles on the left of the road. The church is reached via a track heading up from these.
9. Agios Taxiarchis: the church of the Archangels Michael and Gabriel. This is on the right hand side of the road to Patitiri, just past Ag. Yiannis.
10. Profitis Ilias (Elijah): this is on the left of the road from the Old Village to Patitiri, just before the turning to Yialia.
11. Agios Fanourios: this is a privately owned church on the turning to the OTE towers, now the site of the 'Sunset Café'.
12. Agios Sotiras (Metamorphosis): at Vouno.
13. Church of the Panagia at Vouno: this is a basilica with a cupola, dating from the 16th - 17th century. The church had marvellous frescoes depicting Christ and His apostles until some over-enthusiastic spring cleaning covered them with a layer of asvesti. The celebrations at this church take place on the 23rd August to mark the birth of the Virgin.
14. Agia Paraskevi: the main church in Patitiri.
15. Agios Pantelimonas: in Votsi
16. Agios Petros & Agios Pavlos: a privately-owned church at the Atrium Hotel

MAP OF THE CHURCHES ON ALONNISOS

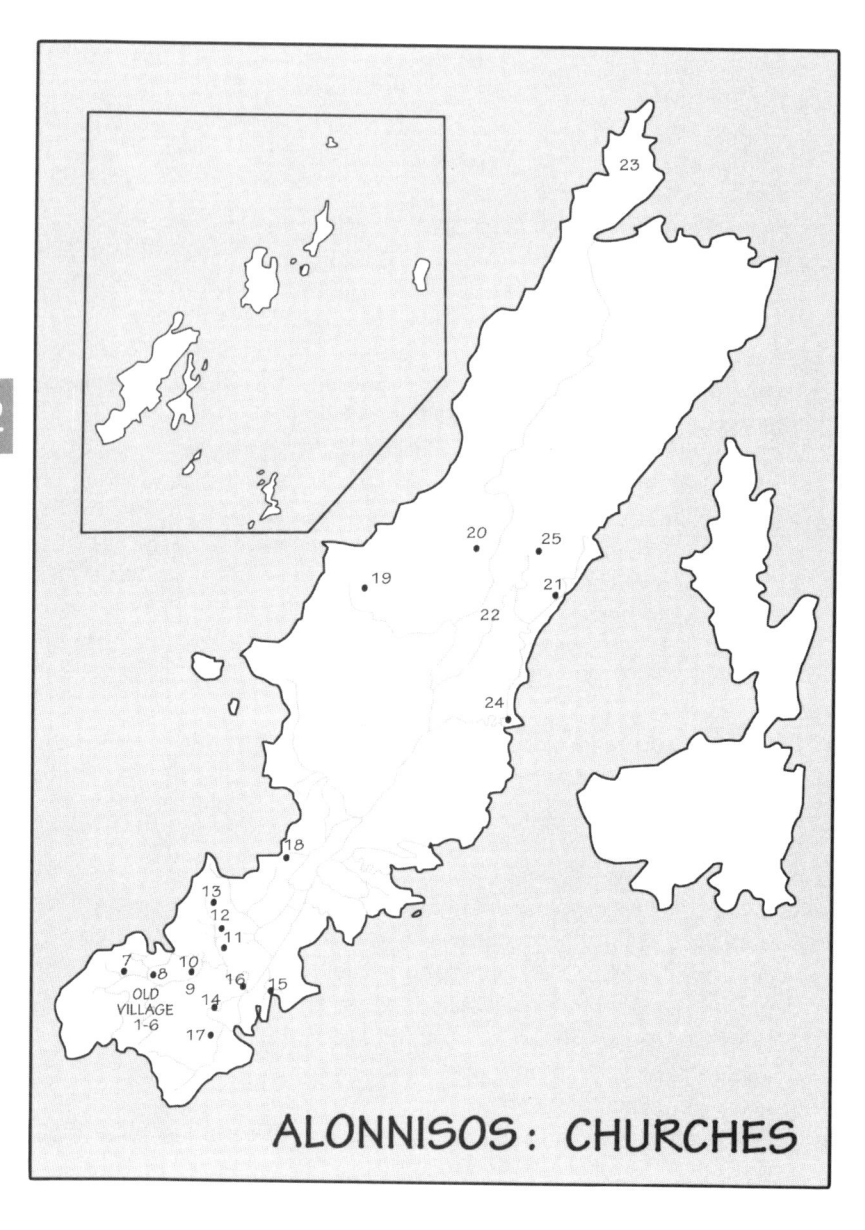

ALONNISOS: CHURCHES

17. Agios Alexandros: Paleochorafina
18. Agii Anargiroi: the churches of the healing Saints, Agios Kosmas and Agios Damianas. The Saints were 4th century Arab doctors who treated the poor in Athens for no charge - Anargiroi means without payment. The old church dates from the 15th - 16th century and has been carefully restored. Formerly there was a monastery on this site and ruins of the cells can still be seen. The newer church was built just after the second world war. The churches are situated above the beach at Tourkoneri, tucked away in the forest and high above the sea.
19. Agios Konstantinos: Psilirachi
20. Agios Yorgos: Khardami
21. Agia Marina: Vamvakies
22. Agios Nektarios: Mourtero
23. Analipsis: near Gerakas
24. Agios Konstantinos: Steni Vala
25. Agios Stephanos: in the grounds of a privately-owned house at Mourtero

The church of Analipsis near Gerakas

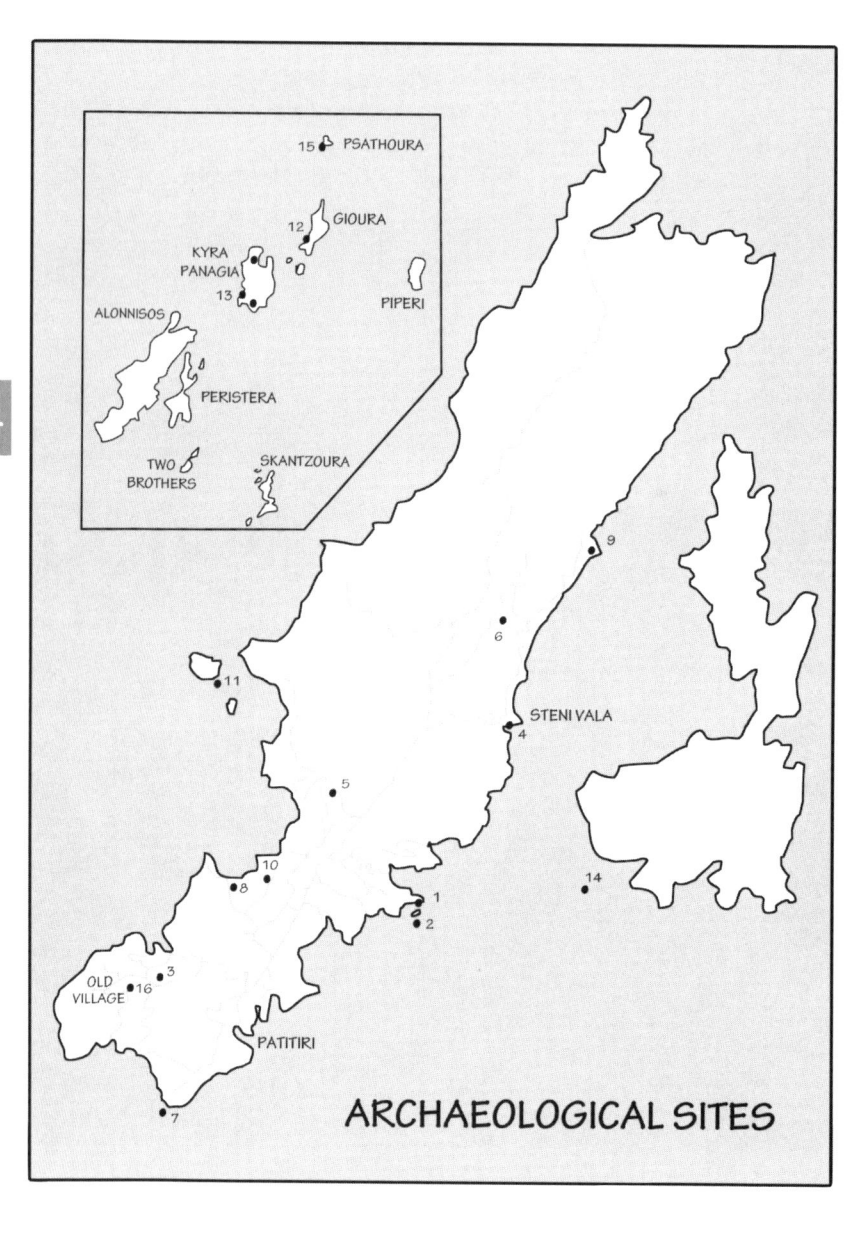

MAP OF ARCHAEOLOGICAL SITES

ARCHAEOLOGICAL SITES

Alonnisos is rich in its ancient history and has a number of sites of archaeological interest. Unfortunately these are poorly delineated and there is very little (or no) information at any of the sites to explain what one is looking at. However, just getting to these sites gives you the opportunity to take in the glorious scenery and imagine that you are standing in the same places that were once populated by very distant ancestors.

1. Kokkinokastro: this is the site of ruins of the city of ancient Ikos and its cemetery, dating from the mesolithic period. During the Classical period, Ikos was fortified with walls – the remains of these can still be seen today, but only from the sea (and only then if you look very closely!). Access to the headland from the beach is not recommended – there have been serious land slippages over the past few years. One of the graves (mnimata) is thought to be that of King Peleus, the father of Achilles.

Excavated walls at ancient Ikos

2. Vrachos: paleolithic remains have been found.
3. Agios Yiannis: remains of an ancient settlement (classical period) were found here, also of a tower. This was thought to be an observation post, as from this hill either side of the island can be seen, as well as the strait between Alonnisos and Skopelos.
4. Steni Vala: ancient buildings and pots have been found.
5. Kastraki: During the Classical period there was a fortified settlement at Kastraki and the remains of a look-out tower are still visible, overlooking the northern sea approach to Alonnisos. Neolithic tools have been discovered here.
6. Garbitses: this was also a look-out tower, overlooking the southern sea approach to the island.
7. Marpounta: remains of a temple have been found on the sea bed, thought to have been dedicated to Aesculapius.

8. Tsoukalia: the back of the beach is littered with potsherds. This is the site of kilns in which wine amphorae were fired. Some pieces of pottery have been found with the inscription 'Ikion' (c 400BC).
9. Agios Dimitrios: the remains of walls of a byzantine basilica have been found behind the 'wetland' area.
10. Agios Andreas: Here, ruins of a byzantine church have been found. From the architectural remains (stone columns with fluting, reliefs), the church is thought to date from the paleochristian period (6th - 7th century AD).
11. Manolas: the remains of an ancient shipwreck have been discovered near this small islet off the north-western coast of Alonnisos
12. Cave of the Cyclops on Gioura: traces of habitation from Classical and Roman times have been found. The cave also boasts stalagmites and stalactites. Gioura is a protected islet and it is forbidden to land here without express permission from the Ministry of the Interior.
13. Kyra Panagia: remains of a neolithic settlement have been found on an islet in the bay of Agios Petros. This is the oldest settlement in the Aegean (6000-5000BC). The largest part of this settlement is underwater at a depth of about 10m. In Byzantine times a monastery dedicated to the Virgin Mary was built at Agios Petros and the ruins of this can still be seen. The remains of two fortified settlements have been identified in the two natural harbours on the island, Agios Petros and Planitis (artefacts and antiquities have been found on the sea bed in the bay at Planitis), thought to have been inhabited from the Classical to the Roman eras.
14. Peristera: In 1984 a shipwreck was discovered off the southern tip of the island by Kostas Mavrikis and reported to the Archaeological Service. The ship is thought to date from 470BC and was carrying more than 3000 amphorae. It had been previously thought that it was not possible to build a ship of this size (approximately 11 tons) during that era. The amphorae were scattered on the sea bed covering an area of 22-30m by 10m. From the position of the amphorae scientists were able to visualise the shape of the ship.
15. Psathoura: the sunken walls of a city have been discovered on the sea bed.
16. Old Village: the walls that surround the 'Kastro' date from byzantine times. In the 13th century they were repaired by the Venetians. The key to the fortress gate (palioporta/paraport) is still on the island.

AGRICULTURE

After the civil war the main occupations of the island were concerned with agriculture. Wheat, barley and maize were all grown for domestic consumption and threshed on the corn circles (Aloni) near the Old Village. The economy of the island depended mainly on the production of wine.

The dry climate and soil quality were ideal for viniculture, and Alonnisos was famous for its red wine. The grapes were very sweet, giving the wine a high alcohol content: locally produced wine was also used to give body and strength to wines from other areas. To improve yield, local growers began experimenting with vines imported from the mainland. Sadly, in 1953, these vines brought phylloxera to the island: this is a plant louse which affects the roots of the vine and kills it. The name is derived from the Greek words for leaf (phyllo) and dry (kseros). The disease spread with amazing speed and wiped out the island's vineyards within 2 years. The destruction of the economic base caused the population to fall dramatically as the young and able moved away from the island in search of work. This left the island populated by the elderly and the very young, depending on remittances from family members working away from the island.

After the decline of the wine industry there was an increase in fishing. In 1962 the fishermen joined forces to create a co-operative, but this was abandoned a few years later due to bad organisation. The co-operative was then re-instituted and, until fairly recently, the day's catch was landed in Patitiri and sold from the co-operative on the harbour front. However, now the fish caught are either used to stock the tavernas run by the families of the fishermen or sold from the fishmonger's opposite the police station. Most of the local fishermen use small boats, although there are some larger trawlers which are indiscriminate in their catch and which damage the sea bed. Government subsidies to fishermen in the form of grants to update engines and equipment, and cheap diesel, resulted in an increase in the number of boats and a decrease in the sizes of both the fish and the catch. Fish stocks diminished due to intensive over-fishing by tratas and gri-gri boats. A dying habit, fortunately, is that of catching fish by dynamiting, although the odd explosion can still be heard. The competition between fishermen and seals for the available fish has led to some seals being killed because of the damage they have done to the nets. In 1992 the National Marine Park of Alonnisos, Northern Sporades (NMPANS) was set up by

Presidential Decree to protect the monk seals and other species while developing the region by the sustainable use of its natural resources. It is immensely gratifying to see that the concept of the Marine Park is now giving results: fish stocks have increased in coastal waters due to the restrictions on fishing and this is resulting in increased sightings of marine mammals close to the shore. The one failure is kalamari: in days gone by, you could see a whole string of boats fishing for kalamari when looking out to sea after dark (kalamari are caught by phosflourescent lures). As a result of over fishing there are now no local kalamari available in tavernas: all the squid available in tavernas are imported to the island and, by law, appear on the menus as 'frozen'.

The silvery green leaves of the olive trees covering the terraced slopes are evocative of Greece. The olive is one of the oldest crops in the world and is believed to have been introduced to this area by the Persians. After washing, the ancient Greeks would rub olive oil into their skin to keep it supple. The olive tree grows quite slowly but may live for more than 1,000 years. It is a member of a large family of trees and shrubs which includes lilac, privet, ash, jasmine and forsythia.

Olive collection

Here, olives are grown for local consumption. In March and April the trees are trimmed and the surrounding land is cleaned and fertilized with lipasma (an organic mixture of nitrogen, phosphorus and potassium). Olives are harvested in October/November, the timing being dependent on the season's rainfall: this is an enterprise which involves the whole family. Tarpaulins are spread on the ground underneath the trees and the olives are knocked off the trees with a long bamboo cane. The olives are then sorted into those which will be processed for eating and those which are to be pressed. Both the immature green and the ripe black olives are inedible before processing. The olives can be prepared for eating in one of two ways: they are either cracked and stored in brine for about 20 days (the brine being changed every 2 days); or alternatively they are packed with lemon and salt and kept in weighted bags for 5-6 days. The island has a co-operative olive press above Leftos Yialos. This only manages the first pressing, so that all the oil produced locally is extra virgin. It used to be the case that a percentage of the oil produced was taken as payment but now money is preferred. The pressed material is shipped to Volos for subsequent pressings, to be made into lower grade oil or soap, and the residue is returned to Alonnisos to fuel the press.

The almond trees have now recovered from a blight which struck them about 20 years ago. Honey production is now also making a comeback after helicopter-spraying of insecticide to eradicate the almond blight also killed the bees. Figs are also grown, and there are many citrus trees: again, this fruit is for local consumption rather than for commercial production.

More and more vines are now being planted: new stock has been imported from California. At present, most of the wine produced is only sufficient for local consumption but some tavernas sell their own wine.

Livestock is popular: many people keep chickens and turkeys, and visitors might even spot the odd goose and duck. There are still several large herds of goats on the island – the sound of the bells in the hills is quite magical. Less magical is the damage that goats en masse can do to a garden, which is why people are quite keen that you close any gates you go through.

Resin collection used to be a thriving business on the island: in the 1950's there used to be 20 resin collectors on Alonnisos but now there is only one. If you are walking through the forest and you suddenly find that your path stops abruptly, it is probable that you have found one of the resin trails. Resin collection is very hard work: a strip of bark is peeled from the trunk of the tree and a collection tin (in other parts of Greece plastic sacks are used instead) is hammered into the tree below the scar. Acid is applied to the top of the scar to encourage the tree to 'bleed'. When the collection tin is full the contents are tipped into large barrels and left to harden. The resin dump is near Raches (on the road to Megali Ammos) although this site has now been co-inhabited by a goat herder and his enormous flock. Please do not be tempted to dip your fingers into the resin in the tins: the resin is incredibly sticky and takes an age to get off. At one time the resin was sent to Halkida on Euboea but now it goes to Athens. After processing it yields turpentine, rosin for stringed instruments, and compounds used in paints, medicines, cleaning and household products, disinfectants and varnishes. And, of course, it is used to give the flavouring for retsina. The tradition of resinating wine is believed to have derived from the practice of sealing amphorae with the waxy resin to avoid deterioration in transit: the flavour then leached into the wine itself and the result became an acquired taste. Another story has it that the flavour was added deliberately to discourage the Turks from stealing the stuff! Most retsina is produced in the Attica region of Greece and, rather surprisingly, its largest market outside of domestic consumption is the UK.

Goats grazing the hillside

OLIVE OIL – A GIFT OF THE GODS

For thousands of years the inhabitants of the Mediterranean countries have cultivated the olive tree and used its products. The olives and the oil produced from these were eaten, both the leaves and the oil were considered to have therapeutic powers and the oil was used as an offering to the gods.

But when did the olive tree first appear? Fossilized leaves have been found on Aegean islands dating back 50 - 60 thousand years. At some point in pre-history man developed a way of cultivating or domesticating the wild olive trees, Olea crysophylla, and this process was thought to have originated in Crete. The archaeological excavations at Ierapetra in Crete discovered information about systemic cultivation of olive trees in the early bronze age (Early Minoan period, 2,800 – 2,100 BC). During that time, people used olive wood for building and, perhaps, for furniture production. Oil lamps found during the Cretan archaeological excavations suggest that olive oil was also used for lighting. 3,500 year old olives were discovered near Zakros – these were thought to have been an offering to the gods before a powerful earthquake which decimated the region.

Human remains dating from 1,500BC have been found with olive stones, suggesting that olives were necessary to accompany the dead into the underworld. Minoan and Mycenaean art from the 3rd millennium BC depict amulets in the shape of olive leaves. Artifacts dating from 2,000 BC depict ideograms for olive trees and oil and tablets found suggest that various aromatic plants were used to scent the oil which was then offered to the gods.

Ideograms symbolising olive oil, the olive tree and the olive itself

The Minoans and the people of the Mycenaean period used olive oil for practical as well as religious purposes. A chemical analysis of a Minoan utensil showed traces of oil used for cooking and tablets found at Knossos record deliveries of oil along with other basic food products.

Other tablets have shown references to scented oil and the names of those who scented the oil were also mentioned – Eumedes, Thyestas, Kokalus and Philaeus were oil scenters from Pylos in the Peloponnese who used aromatics such as rose petals, sage and coriander.

Among other works, Homer wrote two poems containing important information concerning the olive tree and its oil. It is said in the poems that in the gardens of Alkinoos, the king of the Phaeakae, there were olive trees with edible fruit. Homer also wrote that olive wood was used in furniture production: in fact, Odysseus built his bed from olive wood. Scented olive oil was used in caring for the living body as well as the bodies of the dead. Aphrodite was said to have used rose-scented oil when she anointed the dead body of Hector.

In the 5th century BC the Athenians introduced special measures to protect olive trees. Sacred trees were mentioned which were believed to have descended from the very olive tree which the goddess Athena had planted on the acropolis – the very first olive tree to have been planted in the world! Mighty Zeus himself was the protector of the holy trees planted in the 'sacred grove' at Academia.

In the ancient Cretan town of Dreros, close to the modern town of Agios Nikolaos, an ancient inscription was discovered which exhorted every young man to plant at least one olive tree and to look after it until it had fully grown.

During Roman times the use of olive oil became much more widespread and the empire undertook measures to ensure that its citizens did not suffer any shortages. The importation and distribution of oil was closely monitored and large quantities were transported to areas with little or no production. The cultivation of olive trees became a major occupation for the inhabitants of Greece and during the Byzantine period large scale production developed in several areas, particularly the Peloponnese.

OLIVE OIL AS FOOD

The uses of olive oil in cooking were extended during the classical period and complicated forms of cooking were developed to meet the demand for more unusual ideas. Archestratus (an early Heston Blumenthal perhaps?) devised some unusual recipes using fish as well as the more usual use with cheese and vegetables. Two-banded bream was cooked with cheese and olive oil.

Glaucus (a type of sea bass) was boiled in water with spices and olive oil, following which the fish was put in brine. This is according to the recipe which was saved by Oreibasius, a famous doctor during the Byzantine era.

Olive oil was as essential for the cooking of cereals, vegetables and pulses as it still is today. The oil used for cooking and for salad and vegetable dressings was always of a very high standard – today, locally produced oil is what is deemed elsewhere as 'extra virgin'. Our olive press only produces oil from the first pressing. Even sweets are made with olive oil!

In the Christian religion, olive oil is one of the three blessed products. Eusevius, a religious writer of around 335 AD, wrote *...to mankind, who is a civilized animal and honoured by the great god, excellent bread, wine and olive oil were given. The bread supports and strengthens the heart, the wine lightens the spirit and the oil relaxes the body in that it cures and alleviates demanding hardships.* In the Byzantine period, olive oil was accessible to people of all social classes. In the Middle Ages in Constantinople, cooking with oil had reached a very high level and it was during this time that forks first appeared on tables – they were transported to the West around the 10th century, as part of the dowry of Theodora Douka.

Olive oil was one of the special foods which were prohibited during certain Orthodox celebrations. During the Lenten fast neither animal products nor olive oil can be eaten. In fact, the Orthodox Church requires bodily cleansing prior to Christmas and the festival of the Virgin Mary on 15th August too, and in monasteries fasting is required on other days, particularly on Wednesdays and Fridays. Although the consumption of oil is prohibited, olives may be eaten. A 16th century traveller noted that the basic food of the monks on Mount Athos was salted olives, broad beans and greens. Nikos Kazantzakis (of 'Zorba the Greek' fame) described the lives of the hermits who lived in caves .. *a basket is hung near the sea and when a boat passes by, a little bread and some olives are thrown in ... so as not to leave the hermits to die of hunger*

Today, the Cretan diet is considered to be the best example of a Mediterranean diet, with Cretans exhibiting a very low incidence of heart disease and cancer – and a large part of that diet concerns the ingestion of copious quantities of olive oil! The English traveller Robert Pashley, who toured Crete shortly after the revolution of 1821, calculated that each Cretan family consumed four okades (1 oka = 1280g) of olive oil every week. This translates to 350 litres a year! He wrote that the Cretans gave olive oil to their children on bread, with greens and with meat and fish. He also wrote ... *it is the only thing they are liberal with!*

THE USE OF OLIVE OIL FOR LIGHTING

Olive oil has been used for the lighting of houses and public buildings since prehistoric times. In evening ceremonies which required lighting, the role of olive oil was sacred which it still is today. According to Herodotus (5th century BC) there was a special celebration in Egypt which was known as 'lychnokajia' (lighting of the lamps).

THE OLIVE AND ITS OIL AS MEDICINE

A writer in ancient times (Aelianus, 3rd century AD) claimed that olive oil and the olive tree flowers were medicines that could be used even on elephants, so as to pull out the arrows shot by hunters...*when an elephant is injured by many arrow heads, it eats olive tree flowers or oil and then whatever has hurt can be removed. It is at once again strong.* Doctors throughout the ages have mentioned an array of prescriptions which use olive oil as a basic ingredient. It was mainly used as an antipyretic by being rubbed onto the body of the person with a fever but also had its uses as a neurological remedy – doctors recommended bathing in lukewarm olive oil for those with neuralgia.

In fact, olive oil was the panacea for all ills: poisoning, maintaining white teeth, stomach problems, dermatitis and leprosy. Of course, the finest oil for therapeutic purposes was that taken from the oil lamps of the icons. The apostle Mark tells us that Christ's disciples anointed the sick with olive oil to effect a cure.

OLIVE OIL AS AN APHRODISIAC

Folklore medicines used olive oil as an aphrodisiac. Cretan folklore held that the oil was far more effective if it had not been cooked and if it had been produced from wild trees. It was believed that if newly-weds ate bread soaked in the first olive oil of the year, conception would be facilitated. A rather coarse Greek saying extols the aphrodisiac qualities of olive oil while suggesting that those who eat butter instead will just go straight to sleep!

THE OLIVE AND ITS OIL IN WORSHIP

The olive tree impressed prehistoric man because it lived for hundreds of years and almost never dried out: new shoots grew in the dried trunks and so the tree was reborn. In the prehistoric religions of the eastern Mediterranean, men worshipped a young god who died and was reborn every year to coincide with the growth of plants. The religious respect of nature this engendered was extended to the worship of certain trees: an olive tree can be recognised on the sarcophagus of the Agia Triada and the olive tree supposedly planted on the acropolis by Athena was worshipped in Athens in the 5th century BC.

There is much evidence to show that olive branches and leaves were put into graves and it was not unusual that the body was laid on a layer of olive branches. Plutarch (46-127 AD), in his biography of Lykourgos (a law-maker from Sparta c800 BC), wrote of his insistence that the dead must be buried on olive branches.

In ancient times it was common to plant olive trees next to graves, in addition to the cypress pines so often seen near churches and nekrotafia (cemeteries) today. The planting of trees went hand in hand with the hope of rebirth. In some parts of Greece an olive branch was placed next to the graves of hermits: should this branch take root and grow, it was deemed a sure sign of the holiness of whoever lay in the grave.

During celebrations for an abundant harvest, the gods were offered an olive branch in blossom from which was hung fruit, sheep's wool and small flasks containing olive oil, honey and wine. This offering was called an 'eiresioni' and was a show of gratitude for the bountiful earth having provided sustenance for the coming year. Modern Greeks pick olive branches on New Year's Day in the hope of a good harvest. In the Ionian and Aegean islands a special celebration took place once the harvesting had been completed: food was prepared with the newly pressed oil, even though some might have been left from the previous year. Chick pea bread was baked and the table covered with lots of food so that the year would be one of abundance. A special sweet was prepared – olive oil pie – which was made with grape juice and, of course, lashings of olive oil!

Traditionally, for Greeks, the olive tree is the symbol of peace: Irini (Peace – the daughter of Zeus and Themis) is portrayed with an olive branch in her hands. The oil from the lamp of Agios Nikolaos, the patron saint of sailors, is always kept to pour into the sea when it is rough – pouring oil on troubled waters, in fact!

On the Saturday before Holy Week an olive branch is taken into the church. On Palm Sunday, two youths take the branch and lead the priest and worshippers in the procession of the icons around the church: this procession goes round 3 times and finishes in an open area. The Gospel is read in front of the branch and when the phrase 'others cut branches from the trees' is heard the members of the congregation snap off a piece of the branch and take it home with them to protect against various illnesses.

A myth developed over the years to explain why the olive tree had a dry trunk. When Christ was crucified and sadness spread throughout the world, the leaves of all the other trees fell off. Only the olive tree kept its leaves and, when the other trees asked why, the olive tree said 'your leaves have fallen but they will re-grow. My leaves did not fall but my heart knows only too well.' Cretan folklore maintains that when Christ was hunted before His crucifixion He rested under an olive tree and laid His head on its trunk. His tears watered the roots of the tree and, having been watered by the tears of Christ the olive tree is a blessed plant which gives us the most delicious of foods.

In the baptism ceremony in the Orthodox Church, olive oil is the medium through which the grace of God is transferred to the person being baptised. Purification is carried out with water in which drops of olive oil and wine have been poured crosswise. The ceremony starts with the priest anointing the candidate's body with olive oil: after the benediction, crosses are made with olive oil on the forehead, the chest and on the back, in between the shoulder blades.

OLIVE TREES AND OIL IN MYTHOLOGY

Legend has it that Heracles (not the famous Greek hero) first planted an olive tree at Olympia, one which he had brought with him from his home on Crete. He had four brothers and one day he challenged them all to a race. He awarded the winner with a branch from the tree - and so the custom of awarding garlands of olive branches began.

Elais, Spermo and Oino were the granddaughters of Dionysus and Ariadne, born on the Aegean island of Delos. Their names relate to the three main products of the land: the olive, wheat and wine respectively.

The olive tree planted on the acropolis by Athena came about as a contest between herself and Poseidon, when they both wanted to govern the city state of Athens. Each was to offer an invaluable present, the winner to be decided by the other immortals. Poseidon thrust his trident into the side of the acropolis, whereupon a torrent of salty water was released. Athena stabbed her javelin into the same spot and an olive tree immediately flourished: this was deemed to have won the contest. In 480 BC the Persians invaded Athens, took control of the acropolis and burned down the tree. The despair of the Athenians turned to joy when, the next morning, a new shoot was found to be sprouting from the burnt remains of the original tree.

Poseidon was, needless to say, pretty angry at the decision to award victory to Athena and to get even he never allowed Attica to have enough water for its needs. One of his sons, Alirrothios, tried to chop down the tree but the axe slipped in his hand and cut off his leg!

Heracles (the Greek hero this time!) always carried an all-conquering club cut from a wild olive tree he had found near the Saronic Gulf. On touching a statue of Hermes, the messenger of the gods, with his club it miraculously grew roots and leaves.

The old olive press near Gerakas

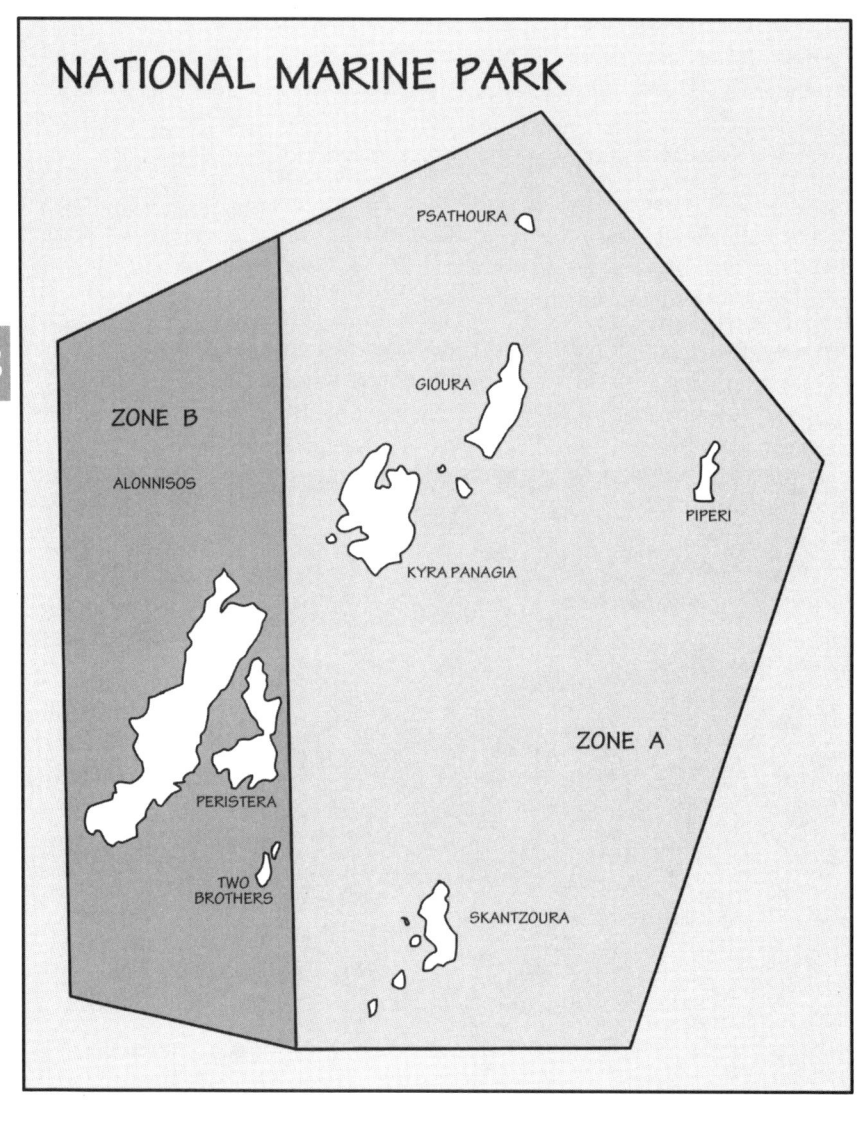

MAP OF THE NATIONAL MARINE PARK OF ALONNISOS - NORTHERN SPORADES (NMPANS)

The olive tree planted on the acropolis by Athena came about as a contest between herself and Poseidon, when they both wanted to govern the city state of Athens. Each was to offer an invaluable present, the winner to be decided by the other immortals. Poseidon thrust his trident into the side of the acropolis, whereupon a torrent of salty water was released. Athena stabbed her javelin into the same spot and an olive tree immediately flourished: this was deemed to have won the contest. In 480 BC the Persians invaded Athens, took control of the acropolis and burned down the tree. The despair of the Athenians turned to joy when, the next morning, a new shoot was found to be sprouting from the burnt remains of the original tree.

Poseidon was, needless to say, pretty angry at the decision to award victory to Athena and to get even he never allowed Attica to have enough water for its needs. One of his sons, Alirrothios, tried to chop down the tree but the axe slipped in his hand and cut off his leg!

Heracles (the Greek hero this time!) always carried an all-conquering club cut from a wild olive tree he had found near the Saronic Gulf. On touching a statue of Hermes, the messenger of the gods, with his club it miraculously grew roots and leaves.

The old olive press near Gerakas

MAP OF THE NATIONAL MARINE PARK OF ALONNISOS - NORTHERN SPORADES (NMPANS)

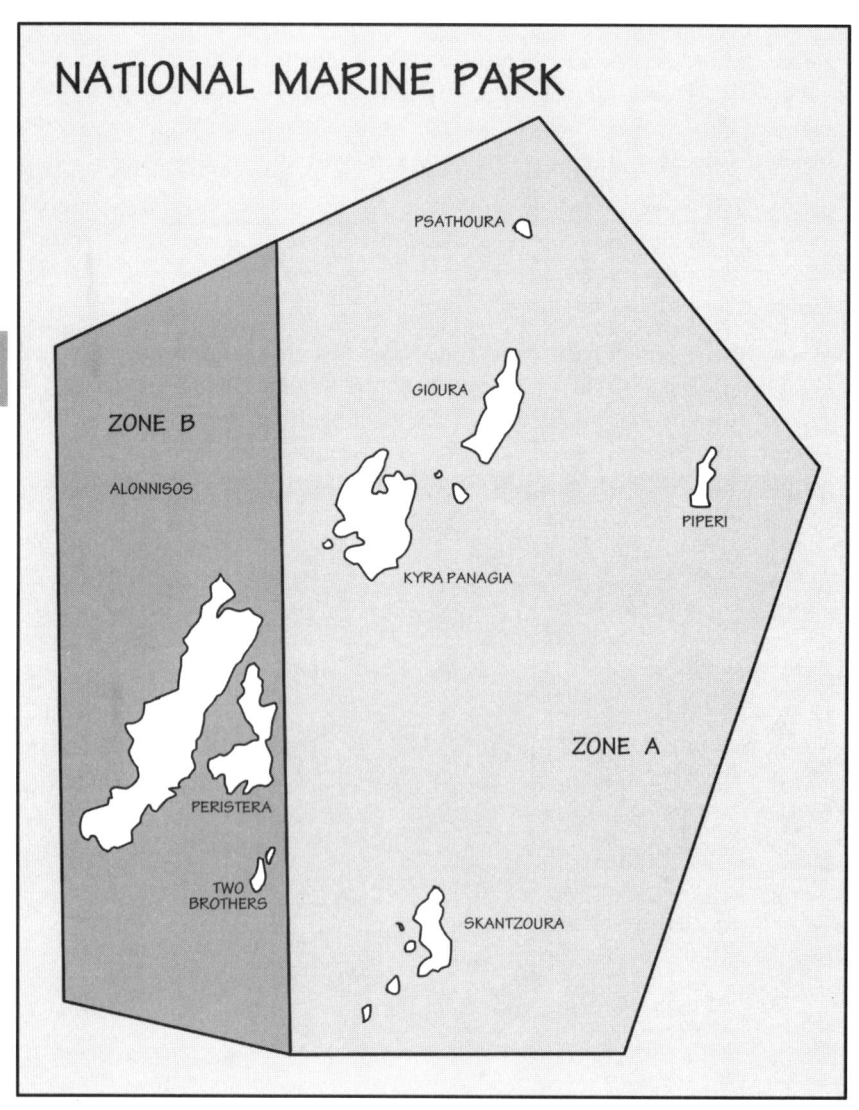

NATIONAL MARINE PARK OF ALONNISOS - NORTHERN SPORADES (NMPANS)

The area was declared a National Marine Park by presidential decree in 1992. The creation of the National Park has the following aims:

- The protection, conservation and management of the wildlife and landscape which constitute natural heritage and a valuable national resource, in terrestrial and marine areas of the N. Sporades
- The protection of one of the most important habitats of the monk seal (Monarchus monarchus) which is a species threatened with extinction
- The protection of other rare and threatened plant and animal species found in these islands
- The development of the region, by the sustainable use of its natural resources

The park is divided into 2 zones. Zone A is strictly protected, the areas in question having been chosen on the basis for the urgency of protection and the uniqueness of flora and fauna species. Zone B includes inhabited areas and protection measures are less stringent.

GEOLOGY

Limestone rock dominates the area. Its main characteristics are the steep rocky slopes, which run down to the sea. The erosion of the limestone by the sea and rainwater has resulted in the formation of caves, which form an important part of the habitat of the monk seal, and aquifers which store water. These sources of fossil water have been seriously depleted over the years by the indiscriminate use of water.

FLORA

The islands are covered in Mediterranean coniferous forest and maccia vegetation such as the strawberry tree (arbutus), lentisc, phyllyrea and holly oak. Species of evergreens include maple, wild olive, the Phoenician juniper and the rare Amelanchier chelmea. Underwater sea-grass beds of the seaweed Poseidonia, which is particularly important for the development of other organisms and the retention and cycling of suspended particles in the marine environment, are widespread.

FAUNA

The area of the park is an important habitat for many species of fish, birds, reptiles and mammals. The Mediterranean monk seal (Monarchus monarchus), red coral (Coralium rubrum), Eleonora's falcon (Falco eleonorae), Audouin's gull (Larus audouinii), shag (Phalacrocorax aristotelis) and the wild goat of Yioura (Capra aegagrus) are some of the rarest species.

Different species of eagle nest on the islands: a pair of Benelli's eagles have been spotted in the Kastana Gorge. Other bird species include cormorants, sheerwaters, gulls and species of the family Sylvidae (eg the Sardinian Warbler and the Blackcap).

Eleonora's Falcon on the wing

Audouin's gulls nest in colonies on small, uninhabited, flat and usually rocky islands. It is a non-migratory species feeding mainly on fish and, less often, on invertebrates, small birds and plants. Worldwide distribution is limited and it nests only in the western part of the Mediterranean and the Aegean. It is estimated that there are about 40 pairs in Greece, with 90% of these in the Marine Park. Man is the bird's greatest threat to survival, but competition with the white gull is also an important factor.

The shag lives exclusively in sea areas, nesting in small colonies, mainly on rocky, uninhabited islands. Its most important habitats in the Aegean are the Marine Park area and the Dodecanese.

Eleonora's falcons nest on rocky islands and their diet consists mainly of insects and small migratory birds. Greece is host to two thirds of the world's population of Eleonora's falcons. The seas of the Marine Park are home to several species of dolphin (striped, common, bottle-nosed) and whale (pilot, sperm). The richness and variety of wildlife and the beautiful scenery characterise the Park as an area of great aesthetic value and biological diversity.

THE MEDITERRANEAN MONK SEAL

Monarchus monarchus has been represented on ancient Greek coins and Homer has described it basking in the sun on sandy beaches. Today, its habitat is restricted to rocky shores and caves on uninhabited islands. It is one of the largest seal species in the world, with a length of 2 to 3 metres and an average weight of 250kg. Its skin is covered by glossy fur, which is most commonly grey or brown on the back and lighter underneath. Newborn pups are about a metre long and weigh 15-20kg. They have a coat of long, wool-like fur and a white spot in the umbilical region. The reproductive period is mainly between the months of May and November and, since the reproductive cycle is a long one (an 11 month gestation period followed by 6-8 weeks lactation) and the female has only one pup at a time, the rate of reproduction is particularly slow. The monk seal feeds on a variety of fish, octopus and squid and its food requirement is about 5% of body weight daily.

Monk seal in Patitiri harbour

In the past, seals have been hunted extensively for their skin and fat. More recently seals were considered to be a natural competitor of fishermen and sometimes they have damaged nets to get food. The increasing incidence of such damage was a direct result of intensive over-fishing by, in particular, gri-gri boats, which not only cause immense depletion of fish stocks by their indiscriminate trawling practices but, in addition, greatly damage the sea bed. It was this competition for the food resources which was the main reason for seals being killed. Fortunately, with current awareness of the value of the species, the frequency of such deaths is on the decline.

Pup mortality is high because the pups are born in areas where human intrusion into their habitat is extensive. Apart from over-fishing, pollution and decreased reproductive success due to restricted renewal of genetic material have also contributed to the 'endangered species' status of the monk seal. It is estimated that only a few hundred individuals remain scattered throughout the Mediterranean and on the shores of the North Atlantic.

The Marine Park, because of its morphology and position, is an ideal habitat for the monk seal. The active participation of the region's fishermen and the Fishing Cooperative of Alonnisos in the protection effort is significant and has largely contributed to the elimination of the deliberate killing of seals in this area.

A BRIEF HISTORY OF THE REGION

The oldest archaeological findings in the region are from the Stone Age, when all the islands of the Northern Sporades were joined to the Pelion peninsula. Tools and petrified bones from the Mesolithic period (100,000–33,000BC) have been found at Kokkinokastro and a Neolithic settlement has been found in the bay of Agios Petros on Kyra Panagia. The first known inhabitants were the Dolopes, a tribe related to the Pelasgi. During the century 500-400BC the islands change hands between the Athenians and the Spartans, several times. The islands then prospered under the influence of Philip of Macedon until in 146BC they were conquered by the Romans.

In the 3rd century AD the inhabitants embraced Christianity. As part of the Byzantine Empire the islands flourished economically and culturally, as witnessed by the number of monasteries and churches built during this period. The uninhabited islands of the Marine Park were important monastic centers and many of them still belong to the monastery of Megisti Lavra of Mount Athos.

After the capture of Constantinople by the crusaders the islands became the property of western feudal lords. After the Ottomans broke up the Byzantine Empire in 1453, the area came under the influence of the Venetians. It was devastated in 1538 by the raids of the Turkish fleet under the command of

Barbarossa. In the 16th century the islands were re-inhabited by a Greek population under Turkish occupation. The inhabitants took part in the pre-revolution uprisings against the Turks and in the revolution of 1821. The treaty of London (1830) included the Northern Sporades in the newly established Greek State.

NMPANS: ZONE A

In areas where it is permitted to approach or land on an island, swimming, observation of the sea bed and amateur filming and photography are allowed. There are specific restrictions on fishing (no gri-gri boats) and it is prohibited to fish with spear guns. Scuba diving, camping and the lighting of fires are also prohibited. Hunting is strictly prohibited, with the exception of Gioura when licences may be granted by the Ministry of the Interior for a controlled cull of the goat population.

KYRA PANAGIA (PELAGOS, ANCIENT HALONNESOS)

This is the largest island in zone A. It is hilly but fertile. There are 2 deep bays: Agios Petros in the south and Planitis in the north, which offer safe, natural harbours to sailors. It is at Agios Petros where the remains of a neolithic settlement have been found, thought to be the oldest settlement in the Aegean (6,000-5,000 BC).

In the 5th century BC the island belonged to the Athenians. In 351BC it was captured by a Skopelitan pirate called Sostratos who was ousted in 346BC by Philip of Macedon. It was handed back to the Athenians, a fact declaimed in speeches by the orators Egisippos and Demosthenes. In 341BC Skopelos retook the island but the Mecedonian navy was dispatched to rout the invaders. In the 1st century AD the Romans governed the island and the geographer Pomponius Melas named it 'Polyaigos', meaning many goats.

This name became corrupted to Pelagos. In Byzantine times a monastery dedicated to the Virgin Mary was built at Agios Petros, the ruins of which can still be seen. This monastery was abandoned and a new one, dedicated to the birth of the Virgin, was built in the post-Byzantine period (c16th century) on the eastern side of the island: this was restored in 1863. This monastery is located high on a rock. There are cells on the northern side of the building and these still offer retreats to those of the Orthodox faith. The basilica is situated in the center of the shaded courtyard. The narthex is at the western side of the church and the original iconostasis has been preserved. In the courtyard there are paleochristian remains of a $6^{th}/7^{th}$ century church. Today there is one monk in residence and the whole island is attached to the monastery of Megisti Lavra of Mount Athos. During the summer months there are excursions to Kyra Panagia which take visitors to the monastery: it is well worth the visit!

The steps leading up to the monastery of the Panagia from Monastery Bay

GIOURA (GERONTIA)

This island is 2 miles northeast of Kyra Panagia. It has an area of 11sq km and its relief is striking with precipitous, rocky shores. Phrygana and holly oak dominate the island which also has a rich avifauna. A species of wild goat is found on Gioura which is found nowhere else: these goats are large animals and, if looked down on, seem to have a cross of lighter coloured hair between their shoulder blades. The main reason for the declaration of the island as a Scientific Research Refuge is the protection of the bird species and the caves which form part of the habitat of the monk seal.

The cave of the Cyclops on the western side of the island, thought to be that described in Homer's Odyssey, is very famous. The entrance is well hidden but the interior boasts huge stalagmites and stalactites. Traces of habitation from the Roman and Classical eras have been found. According to tradition, the ancient Romans sent their convicts here.

It is forbidden to approach the island closer than 400m, to land on the island without express permission from the Ministry of the Interior or to drive a boat at speeds of 10mph closer than 2 nautical miles from the coast.

There are several small islets between Gioura and Kyra Panagia. Most of these are dry and infertile, but Pappou has a large hare population and a small church dedicated to the Panagia.

PIPERI

This is 6 miles from Gioura with an area of 7sq km. It was thought to have been inhabited in ancient times as it was very fertile with a good geographical location. From its peaks the Macedonian coast and the whole of the northern Aegean can be seen. A cloister dedicated to the Virgin Mary can be found on the island.

Today, the island of Piperi is the core of the Marine Park and is strictly protected. No vessel is allowed to approach closer than 3 nautical miles. These restrictions are to protect the most important part of the habitat of the monk seal, the birds of prey which nest on the island and the rare species of plants. There are 33 species of birds which nest on Piperi and it is estimated that the island is home to about 350-400 pairs of Eleonora's falcons.

SKANTZOURA

This is a flat island with an even relief. The series of low hills ends on shores of white marble, which used to be quarried. The island is covered in maccia vegetation and phrygana and there is a forest of low cedars. Skantzoura and the nearby rocky outcrops of Strongilo and Polemika constitute an important habitat for the Audouin's gull and Eleonora's falcon. There is a ruined monastery in the centre of the island which was also attached to the Megisti Lavra monastery on Mount Athos.

PSATHOURA

This is the north-easternmost point of the Marine Park. It is a small, flat island of volcanic origin, about 1.5sq km in area, and may be visited freely. The landscape is fairly barren, predominantly lentisc and heather, but there are species of plant here which are not seen anywhere else in the Marine Park – the sea lily, hemlock and brooms. In the south of the island the white sands of Mandraki contrast the black rocks of andesite. In the east are the remains of an ancient sunken city – this was thought to have been a settlement of fishermen as the terrain would not sustain any cultivation. In the north of the island is a large lighthouse, built in 1895 by French engineers: this signals to the international shipping routes of the northern Aegean.

The rare Pancratium maritinum lily found on Psathoura

NMPANS: ZONE B

ALONNISOS
This island was known as Ikos in ancient times and Liadromia in the 16th century. It is the only permanently inhabited island in the Marine Park: the presence on man on the other islands of zone B is limited to seasonal shepherds and farmers. Patitiri is the largest community on the island. Its name derives from the Greek word for wine press. This village only came into being when the earthquake of 1965 made houses in the Old Village uninhabitable and the population was forced to move to the new harbour.

DIO ADELPHIA (TWO BROTHERS)
These 2 small islands, 5 nautical miles from Patiriri, are fairly inhospitable – except to snakes!

PERISTERA (XIRO)
Peristera (the name means seagull) is inhabited seasonally by shepherds and those who stay on the island to harvest their olives (October/November) or trim the trees before the new season's fruit ripens (March).

An ancient shipwreck has been discovered off the southern coast of Peristera and this has been researched by the Hellenic Archaeological Service: the accommodation used by the divers can still be seen. In years gone by there were chromium mines on the island but these fell into disuse after the Second World War. Vasiliko bay offers a very safe, natural harbour for yachts. Inlets around the coastline have, over the years, offered a safe haven to various pirates such as Jelios, after whom one such bay is named. A small island to the north of Peristera in named Lechousa, because its shape is reminiscent of a reclining pregnant lady.

Although now only seasonally inhabited it appears that this was not always the case; many tombs have been found. During the Byzantine period the island was called Sarakonisi (island of the Saracens). In 904AD the Saracens plundered Thessaloniki and then took shelter in Vasiliko. Among the ships was one full of women and children, destined to be sold as slaves: for the 3 days that the ships were in Vasiliko, the lamentations of these unfortunates could be heard by the whole of Alonnisos and this prompted the change of name to Sarakonisi.

Peristera

A.S.A.P.

Feeding time...

ALONNISOS SOCIETY FOR ANIMAL PROTECTION

Whether you are an animal lover or not, visitors to many parts of Greece can't help but be moved by the plight of stray animals. Throughout the country there are differing degrees of neglect, indifference, abuse or abject cruelty. We have recently set up a registered charity on the island - ASAP (Alonnisos Society for Animal Protection) – which is committed to neuter and care for animals, whether pets or strays. We have no vet here, but have been fortunate enough to receive the backing of various other charities which send us locum vets whenever possible and supply us with educational material to help people better comprehend a range of issues, from the benefits of neutering to the hideousness of indiscriminate poisoning. We also arrange for a vet to come from Volos every 2–3 months and it has been very gratifying that so many people bring their animals along to his clinic.

The aim of the society is the promotion of respect for pets, stray animals and the natural environment and the raising of public awareness with respect to their care. It is the belief of the society that the following would be effective ways to achieve its aims and enhance the lives of animals on Alonnisos:

1. The provision of information on how to prevent cruelty to animals whether by neglect, abandonment, violence or the administration of noxious substances.
2. Caring for stray animals, in conjunction with the local council, by feeding or arranging adoption.
3. The instigation of a neutering programme to maintain a healthy, controlled stray animal population.
4. The arrangement of regular visits by veterinary surgeons to care for sick or injured animals and to offer advice on their diet and general well-being.
5. The rendering of first aid to sick or injured animals until such time that veterinary attention can be arranged.

The annual fee for membership of ASAP is 15 euros: this will give you an invitation to the AGM, several newsletters, and the gratitude of the animals of Alonnisos. Check out our web site, www.asap-animalz.org.

USEFUL CONTACTS

Alonnisos web site: www.alonnisos.gr

Holiday companies:
Sunvil Holidays   www.sunvil.co.uk
Greek Islands Club   www.greekislandsclub.com
Ionian/Aegean   www.ionianislandholidays.com
Thalpos   www.holidayislands.com
Manos   www.ThomasCook.com
Olympic Holidays   www.OlympisHolidays.com

KTEL (state bus company)   www.ktelvolou.gr
Athens   210   8329585/8317186
Volos   24210 33254/25527
Thessaloniki   2310   595424

Room rental association of Alonnisos   24240 66188 fax 65577

Hellenic Monk Seal Society (MoM)   www.mom.gr

Diving
Ikion   www.ikion.gr
Poseidonas   diveposeidonas@yahoo.com

Walking on Alonnisos
                                                   www.alonnisoswalks.co.uk
Abcrox   www.abcrox.co.uk

Museum (Angela and Kostas Mavrikis)   24240 66250

Taxis
Spiros Florous   6932 391026
Nikos Athanassiou   6972 250295
Giorgos Athanassiou   6944 564393
Pericles Agallou   6944 564432

Tourist companies

Alonnisos Travel	24240 66000	www.alonnisostravel.gr
Albedo Travel	24240 65804	www.albedotravel.com

Flying Cat/dolphin/ferry tickets

Athens	Alkyon Travel 210 3832545	www.alkyontravel.com
Volos	Vis Travel 24210 31059	www.gtp.gr/VIS-travel
Ag. Konstantinos	Alkyon Travel 22350 31920	www.alkyontravel.com
Ag. Konstantinos	Bilalis Travel 22350 31614	www.bta.gr
Alonnisos	Alkyon Travel 24240 65220	www.alkyontravel.com

Vehicle Hire

Alonnisos Travel (cars, boats)	www.alonnisostravel.gr
Albedo Travel (cars, motorbikes)	www.albedotravel.com
Alkyon Travel (cars)	24240 65220
Venus (cars)	24240 65798
Apollo (cars)	24240 66498
National Alamo (cars)	24240 22198
Maria Vafini (cars, motorbikes)	24240 66174
Dimitris Malamatenios (motorbikes, boats)	24240 65059
IM Bikes (Maria Vlaikou: motorbikes)	24240 65010
S Bikes (Ilias Papanikolaou: motorbikes, boats)	24240 65651
Moto Orizon (motorbikes)	24240 65820
Oasis (Spiros Malamatenios: motorbikes)	24240 65098

Maps

Anavasi	www.anavasi.gr